THE WORLD IN ONE DAY

THE WORLD
IN ONE DAY

Written by
RUSSELL ASH

DK PUBLISHING, INC.

A DK PUBLISHING BOOK

If all the letters sent in one day were stacked together, they would form a bridge that could span the Atlantic Ocean. Find out how many letters this is on page 27.

Senior Art Editor Dorian Spencer Davies
Art Editor Joanna Pocock
Project Editor Linda Sonntag
Managing Editor Sarah Phillips
Senior Managing Art Editor Peter Bailey
US Editor Kristin Ward
Production Charlotte Traill
DTP Designer Karen Nettelfield

First American Edition, 1997
2 4 6 8 10 9 7 5 3 1
Published in the United States by
DK Publishing, Inc
95 Madison Avenue
New York, New York 10016

Visit us on the World Wide Web at
http://www.dk.com

ISBN 0-7894-2028-7

Reproduced in Great Britain by Dot Gradations Limited, Essex
Printed and bound in Italy by A. Mondadori Editore, Verona

The day featured throughout this book is not any particular one, but a typical day in the late 1990s. Of course, there may be certain days when fewer babies are born, or more rice is harvested, for example, but such figures, like all those that follow, are based on daily averages that have been calculated from authoritative statistics for longer periods.

CONTENTS

Turn to page 29 to find out how many people travel each day by the world's top ten airlines.

Turn to page 23 to find out how many tires, refrigerators, washing machines, and planks of wood are produced in the world each day, and how much laundry detergent, steel, and string is produced.

A DAY AROUND THE WORLD

WHAT HAPPENS IN ONE DAY in the life of the world? In the next 24 hours, the world will spin once on its axis and travel more than 1.5 million miles (2.5 million km) in its orbit around the Sun. As they hurtle through space, 2.5 billion people will spend the day at work, and 1 billion children will go to school. But what else is going on? This book gives you the figures for many of the other things that happen in an average day, from how much water an elephant drinks and how many times a flea can jump, to how many potatoes are harvested and how much gold is made into false teeth. So fasten your seat belt as we lift off into the bizarre world of real facts. Enjoy it, and remember . . . tomorrow is another day.

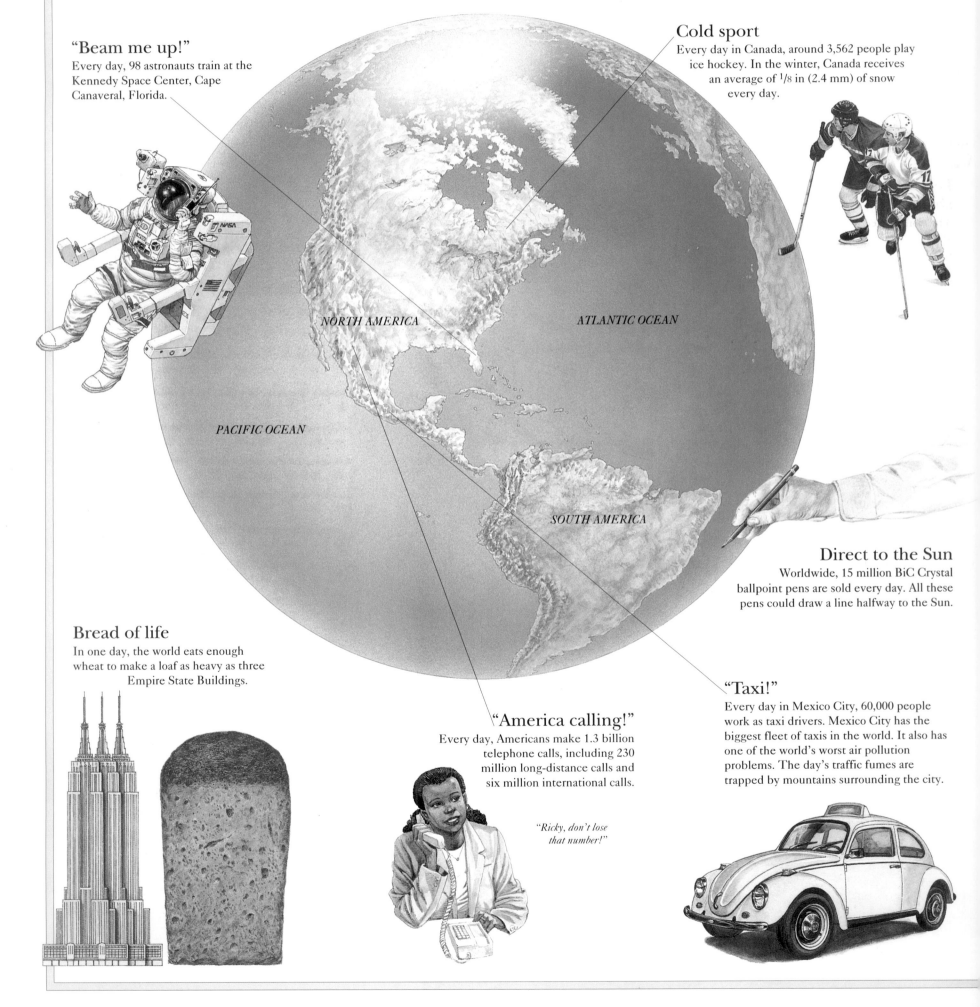

"Beam me up!"
Every day, 98 astronauts train at the Kennedy Space Center, Cape Canaveral, Florida.

Cold sport
Every day in Canada, around 3,562 people play ice hockey. In the winter, Canada receives an average of 1/8 in (2.4 mm) of snow every day.

NORTH AMERICA

ATLANTIC OCEAN

PACIFIC OCEAN

SOUTH AMERICA

Direct to the Sun
Worldwide, 15 million BiC Crystal ballpoint pens are sold every day. All these pens could draw a line halfway to the Sun.

Bread of life
In one day, the world eats enough wheat to make a loaf as heavy as three Empire State Buildings.

"America calling!"
Every day, Americans make 1.3 billion telephone calls, including 230 million long-distance calls and six million international calls.

"Ricky, don't lose that number!"

"Taxi!"
Every day in Mexico City, 60,000 people work as taxi drivers. Mexico City has the biggest fleet of taxis in the world. It also has one of the world's worst air pollution problems. The day's traffic fumes are trapped by mountains surrounding the city.

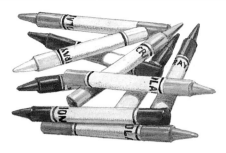

Waxing colorful
Crayola Crayons produces 5 million crayons worldwide every day. Children in the UK spend 3.5 million hours a day drawing and coloring.

Fishy story
Every day in Iceland, 15,000 people go to sea in fishing trawlers, or work in the fish processing industry.

For better or worse
Every day in China, 26,000 couples get married. The average age for people to marry in China is 30.

Military jobs
1.3 million people work every day in the armed forces of the Russian Federation, including 460,000 in the army, 190,000 in the navy and 145,000 in the air force.

Feeling sheepish
The world's sheep yield 5,500 tons (5,000 tonnes) of wool a day. That's enough to make 15.5 million sweaters, one for each person in the Netherlands.

EUROPE

AFRICA

ASIA

Booming city
Tokyo-Yokohama, in Japan, is the biggest continuous urban area, with a population of 28 million. Every day, the population here grows by 819 inhabitants.

INDIAN OCEAN

Drink of the gods
The French produce 16,500 tons (15,000 tonnes) of wine every day. That's 20 million bottles a day!

AUSTRALIA

Plenty of cotton
The world harvests 57,000 tons (52,000 tonnes) of cotton in one day. That's enough to make 207 million T-shirts – one for every inhabitant of Indonesia.

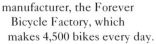

Flying kangas from down under
Every day, 2,624 people work for Qantas, Australia's national airline company.

Steamy work
Every day, 1.6 million people go to work for Indian Railways, the biggest nongovernmental employer in the world.

Snakes alive!
Every day in Sri Lanka, an average of two people are killed by poisonous snakes. Sri Lanka's most common killer snake is the saw-scaled or carpet viper, one of the most poisonous snakes in the world.

On their bikes
The people of Shanghai, in China, make 2.5 million bicycle trips every day. Shanghai also has the world's largest bicycle manufacturer, the Forever Bicycle Factory, which makes 4,500 bikes every day.

PLANET EARTH

SINCE IT CAME INTO BEING ABOUT 4.6 billion years ago, Earth has continued to evolve every day. Heat from the Earth's core forces molten material to bubble to the surface in volcanoes. The plates that form the hard outer layers of the Earth grind against one another. The enormous pressure they exert pushes mountain ranges gradually higher, pulls the continents apart, and causes tremors and earthquakes. Wind, ice, and water wear away at rock. Earth's landscape is steadily changing day by day.

In a flash

Lightning strikes somewhere on Earth 100 times a second. A lot of it zigzags straight into the sea or hits icecaps or huge uninhabited areas of land, so the chances of getting struck by lightning are quite remote. The odds are higher in the tropics, where 3,200 electric storms rend the air every 12 night hours.

Powering Nicaragua by tropical storms

Lightning power

If the power of all the tropical storms that take place in 24 hours could be harnessed, it would be equal to a full year's electricity consumption in a small country like Nicaragua.

Nightly fireworks

Stromboli is a volcano that has been active every day for thousands of years. The ancients called it the Lighthouse of the Mediterranean because it produces a spectacular display of sizzling bombs and red fountains of lava against the night sky.

Volcanic energy

The energy released in one day by the eruption of Mount Tambora was thought to be 16,000 megatons – making it 800,000 times as powerful as the Hiroshima atom bomb.

Great balls of fire

Mount Vesuvius erupted in AD 79. Lava exploded into the air as ash and buried Pompeii. Its inhabitants were asphyxiated by poisonous gases. Ash then mixed with rain to create hot mud flows (lahars), which buried Herculaneum in just one day. The lethal lahars would have kept up with a modern Italian trying to escape on a moped.

Mount Stromboli could go on erupting for hundreds of years before it becomes dormant and finally extinct.

The Bering Glacier in the Arctic began to retreat in the 1980s, raising fears about global warming. In 1993 it started to advance again.

"I'm burning rubber! Hey! Get this lahar off my tail!"

Earth in orbit

Planet Earth spins so fast on its axis that a person standing on the Equator is actually traveling at 1,038 mph (1,670 kmh) – the speed of the Concorde – without moving at all.

Jupiter	Saturn	Neptune	Uranus	Earth	Mars	Pluto	Mercury	Venus
9h 55m	10h 39m	16h 7m	17h 14m	24h	24h 37m	6 days 9h	58 days 14h	244 days

The ice advances

Most glaciers are slow movers. They grind forward by about 6 ft (2 m) a day. The Bering Glacier in the Arctic is an exception. It advances an astonishing 300 ft (91 m) every day. It could transform a large backyard into a skating rink overnight.

How long is a day?

A day on Earth lasts 24 hours, but a day on Venus lasts eight Earth months, because Venus spins so slowly. Jupiter spins so fast that a day flashes by in under 10 hours. An Earth watch would have to lose 2 minutes an hour to keep time on the Moon.

Cosmic dust

Every day 121 tons of cosmic dust – debris from outer space – enters Earth's atmosphere. If it could all be shoveled into one heap, it would be as big as a two-story house.

Powering the
US by hurricane

America by storm
In one day, a hurricane could produce enough energy to replace the whole of the US's electricity supply for nine months.

A day's work for the Sun
Every day the Sun beams 4 trillion kilowatt hours of energy to Earth. This recycles Earth's water by evaporation, causes winds, waves, and ocean currents, and is used in photosynthesis.

Squeaky clean
Enough rain falls to Earth every day for each one of its inhabitants to have a bath every five minutes.

Wet, wet, wet
If all the moisture in Earth's atmosphere fell as rain, it would produce 300 cu miles (1,250 cu km) of water. If all this rain fell in one day on the island of Manhattan, it would submerge it to a depth of 12,500 miles (20,000 km).

SMALL WORLD
Biosphere 2 is a huge greenhouse built in Arizona. Inside the Biosphere are areas of farmland, rain forest, desert, and even an ocean. This is the home of an experiment in global warming. Levels of carbon dioxide (CO_2) in Earth's atmosphere are rising. Scientists will steadily pump more CO_2 into the Biosphere in order to predict Earth's future.

Solar energy
It would take 167,000 nuclear power stations to produce the amount of energy that the Sun beams down to Earth in one day.

When the wind blows
Erosion is the wearing away and removal of land surfaces by running water, wind, or ice. Erosion is greatest in sloping areas and areas of little or no surface vegetation. On the west coast of Mauritania near Nouakchott, prevailing easterly winds carry 767,000 tons of sand and dust from the Sahara Desert into the Atlantic Ocean every day.

Cold snout
The end of a glacier is called the snout. At the snout, the ice either melts as fast as it arrives, or the glacier calves – bits break off to form icebergs. Jakobshavn Glacier in Greenland discharges 20 to 30 million tons of ice a day to the fjord at its snout.

Sand from the Sahara blows into the Atlantic from the west coast of Africa.

Icebergs calve at the snout of Jakobshavn Glacier in Greenland.

A raging torrent
The Iguaçu Falls are a string of 275 waterfalls on the border between Argentina and Brazil, close to Paraguay. The water of the Iguaçu River cascades down spectacular drops of up to 230 ft (70 m). At times of peak flow, enough water passes over the Falls to fill six Olympic swimming pools every second. However, in some years rainfall is so slight that this great river can dry up completely, as it did in 1978.

The Earth moves
An earthquake happens when rocks move along faults. Earthquakes are especially powerful when the tectonic plates that form the Earth's outer layers move against one another. The Great African Rift Valley in Djibouti experiences dozens of earthquakes every day, indicating the continuous movement of the tectonic plates beneath Africa.

A DAY TO REMEMBER

Up to your ears
The wettest day ever was March 15, 1952, when 74 in (190 cm) of torrential rain fell at Cilaos on the island of La Réunion in the Indian Ocean.

Taking a beating
On July 14, 1953, golf ball-sized hailstones fell in a freak storm in Alberta, Canada. Powered by gale-force winds, they bashed to death 36,000 ducks.

Buried
The biggest snowfall ever was recorded on February 7, 1963, when 78 in (198 cm) of snow fell at Mile 47 Camp, Cooper River Division, Alaska.

Sunny side up
On September 13, 1922, the temperature in the shade at al'Aziziyah in the Libyan desert reached 136°F (57.8°C) – hot enough to fry an egg on a rock.

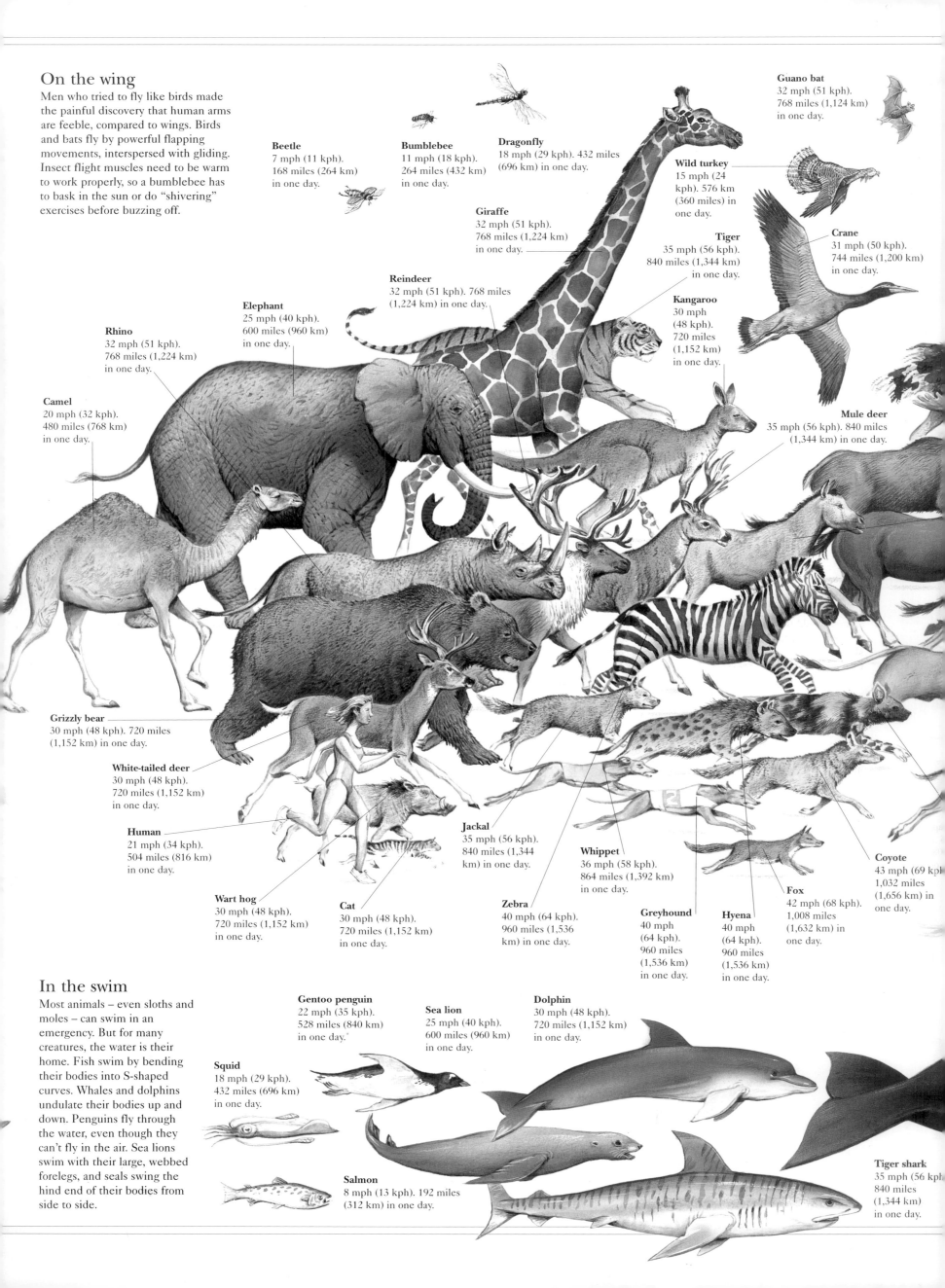

On the wing

Men who tried to fly like birds made the painful discovery that human arms are feeble, compared to wings. Birds and bats fly by powerful flapping movements, interspersed with gliding. Insect flight muscles need to be warm to work properly, so a bumblebee has to basks in the sun or do "shivering" exercises before buzzing off.

Guano bat
32 mph (51 kph). 768 miles (1,124 km) in one day.

Beetle
7 mph (11 kph). 168 miles (264 km) in one day.

Bumblebee
11 mph (18 kph). 264 miles (432 km) in one day.

Dragonfly
18 mph (29 kph). 432 miles (696 km) in one day.

Wild turkey
15 mph (24 kph). 576 km (360 miles) in one day.

Giraffe
32 mph (51 kph). 768 miles (1,224 km) in one day.

Tiger
35 mph (56 kph). 840 miles (1,344 km) in one day.

Crane
31 mph (50 kph). 744 miles (1,200 km) in one day.

Reindeer
32 mph (51 kph). 768 miles (1,224 km) in one day.

Kangaroo
30 mph (48 kph). 720 miles (1,152 km) in one day.

Elephant
25 mph (40 kph). 600 miles (960 km) in one day.

Rhino
32 mph (51 kph). 768 miles (1,224 km) in one day.

Mule deer
35 mph (56 kph). 840 miles (1,344 km) in one day.

Camel
20 mph (32 kph). 480 miles (768 km) in one day.

Grizzly bear
30 mph (48 kph). 720 miles (1,152 km) in one day.

White-tailed deer
30 mph (48 kph). 720 miles (1,152 km) in one day.

Human
21 mph (34 kph). 504 miles (816 km) in one day.

Jackal
35 mph (56 kph). 840 miles (1,344 km) in one day.

Whippet
36 mph (58 kph). 864 miles (1,392 km) in one day.

Coyote
43 mph (69 kph). 1,032 miles (1,656 km) in one day.

Wart hog
30 mph (48 kph). 720 miles (1,152 km) in one day.

Cat
30 mph (48 kph). 720 miles (1,152 km) in one day.

Zebra
40 mph (64 kph). 960 miles (1,536 km) in one day.

Greyhound
40 mph (64 kph). 960 miles (1,536 km) in one day.

Hyena
40 mph (64 kph). 960 miles (1,536 km) in one day.

Fox
42 mph (68 kph). 1,008 miles (1,632 km) in one day.

In the swim

Most animals – even sloths and moles – can swim in an emergency. But for many creatures, the water is their home. Fish swim by bending their bodies into S-shaped curves. Whales and dolphins undulate their bodies up and down. Penguins fly through the water, even though they can't fly in the air. Sea lions swim with their large, webbed forelegs, and seals swing the hind end of their bodies from side to side.

Gentoo penguin
22 mph (35 kph). 528 miles (840 km) in one day.

Sea lion
25 mph (40 kph). 600 miles (960 km) in one day.

Dolphin
30 mph (48 kph). 720 miles (1,152 km) in one day.

Squid
18 mph (29 kph). 432 miles (696 km) in one day.

Salmon
8 mph (13 kph). 192 miles (312 km) in one day.

Tiger shark
35 mph (56 kph). 840 miles (1,344 km) in one day.

ANIMALS

A LOUD CHORUS OF birdsong shakes the animal kingdom from its slumber as the first rays of the Sun touch the treetops. An animal's day centers around key survival activities: defending territory, hunting or foraging for food, and feeding young. Mammals, birds, and winged insects also spend time grooming to keep their bodies clean and healthy. Monkeys and apes groom each other to cement friendships; a cow may indulge in 180 bouts of grooming in one day!

Hummingbird
Up to 5,400 wingbeats a minute.

Bat
Up to 1,200 wingbeats a minute.

Sparrow
600 wingbeats a minute.

Butterfly
Up to 640 wingbeats a minute.

Swift
360 wingbeats a minute.

Stork
180 wingbeats a minute.

In a flap

Most birds, insects, and bats need to beat their wings rapidly in order to stay in the air. A hummingbird's wings beat so quickly you can hardly see them.

Pygmy shrew
Up to 2 million heartbeats a day.

Mouse
720,000 heartbeats a day.

Elephant
43,200 heartbeats a day.

Frog
43,200 heartbeats a day.

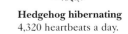

Rabbit
288,000 heartbeats a day.

Hedgehog
432,000 heartbeats a day.

Hedgehog hibernating
4,320 heartbeats a day.

Heartbeats

Surprisingly, all mammals other than humans have around 800 million heartbeats in a lifetime. An elephant's heart beats 20–30 times a minute, so it will have "used up" its heartbeats after about 50 years. At the other end of the scale, a pygmy shrew's heart beats 900–1,400 times a minute; its life span is about 1.5 years.

On the run

Animals run to escape predators and to chase prey. This race of slowpokes and speedy creatures shows how far animals could travel *if* they were able to sprint along at their top speeds for a whole 24 hours.

Three-toed sloth
360 ft (110 m) per hour. 2 miles (3 km) in one day.

Yellow-bellied sea snake
2 mph (3 kph). 48 miles (77 km) in one day.

Giant tortoise
1,214 ft (370 m) per hour. 29,136 ft (8,880 m) per day.

Rosy boa
0.2 mph (0.3 kph). 5 miles (7 km) in one day.

Pig
11 mph (18 kph). 264 miles (432 km) in one day.

Squirrel
12 mph (19 kph). 288 miles (463 km) in one day.

Wild turkey
15 mph (24 kph). 744 miles (1,200 km) in one day.

Common shrew
3 mph (5 kph). 72 miles (116 km) in one day.

Chicken
9 mph (15 kph). 216 miles (348 km) in one day.

Animal appetites

For some creatures, eating is hard work. The African elephant spends about 18 hours out of 24 feeding and drinking. The giant anteater chomps its way through 30,000 ants in one day, and the sperm whale swallows a whole ton of squid. Others just sit back and let food come to them. Moles, for example, feed on unsuspecting passersby that drop into their tunnels.

Vampire bat
Drinks 2 tablespoons of blood every day, the equivalent of half its own body weight.

Mole
Eats its own weight (2–3 oz/ 50–80 g) of food every day.

Anteater
Eats more than 30,000 ants in one day.

Giant panda
Eats 22–99 lb (10–45 kg) of bamboo shoots in one day.

Bull elephant
Eats 500 lb (227 kg) of foliage in one day. Drinks 18–35 gallons (80–160 liters) of water.

Blue whale
Absorbs 4 tons (5 tonnes) of krill (tiny crustaceans) in one day.

PLANTS

WITHOUT PLANTS, THERE WOULD BE no animal life on Earth. Plants produce oxygen, which all creatures need to breathe and to convert food into energy. Their fruits, leaves, and seeds give us food and medicines. Their fibers are woven into clothes. Their juices give us drinks and dyes. Trunks and branches provide shelter, fuel, and material for furniture and tools. So far, we have identified 500,000 plants, and still more await discovery. Yet large areas of natural vegetation are disappearing. Every day, 89,000 acres (36,000 hectares) of tropical rain forest are destroyed. But just one Amazonian Brazil nut tree can produce more nutritious food than can be cultivated on the land that is cleared when the tree is felled.

Plant growth

Plants harness energy from the Sun's rays, turning it into glucose, which they use to grow. This process is called photosynthesis. A large rain forest tree can produce 3 lb (1.5 kg) of pure glucose in one day, using just sunlight and water. Some plants, like those on the left, grow very quickly. Compared with these plants, even the fastest trees seem to grow slowly. Some of the slowest growing plants are lichens (see bottom right), which can take a century to grow just 1 in (2.5 cm).

Morning glory

Morning glory flowers last only one day. They open in the morning and shrivel and die toward evening. Plants flower by responding to the number of hours of daylight in a day. A light-sensitive pigment in the leaves sends a hormone signal to the flower buds, triggering them to open.

Giant bamboo

A native of Burma, the giant bamboo can grow an astonishing 18 in (46 cm) a day. Bamboo is technically a grass. Its stems are used for making buckets, rafts, and chopsticks. In India and Southeast Asia, the bamboo harvest is turned into 5,291 tons of paper a day.

Giant kelp

Giant kelp is a huge seaweed found in the coastal waters of California. It grows up to 18 in (45 cm) per day. Fronds of kelp form underwater forests, and can reach 328 ft (100 m), making it the tallest plant in the world.

Callie grass

Callie grass grows 6 in (15 cm) in one day.

Titan arum

The center of the titan arum shoots up 3 in (7.5 cm) in a day. Its flowers last just one day, giving off a stench of rotting flesh. In its native Sumatra, the titan arum is known as the "corpse flower."

Eucalyptus deglupta

This eucalyptus is the world's fastest growing tree. It can spurt 1 in (2.5 cm) in a day. One specimen in New Zealand reached 35 ft (10.6 m) in 15 months.

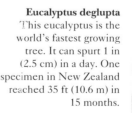

SMALL WORLD

The Royal Botanic Gardens at Kew, near London, UK, house 40,000 living plants, including a growing example of one in 8 of all known flowers, and over 6 million dried plants (9 out of 10 of all species). This is the largest collection of plants in the world. Many of the plants grow in one of several greenhouses at Kew. The greenhouses re-create the conditions of different climates from around the world, ranging from hot desert to cold alpine. Many visitors to Kew feel like they have traveled the globe in just one day.

Giant puffball

The giant puffball fungus can measure up to 6.6 ft (2m) in circumference, and weigh up to 44 lb (20 kg). If an animal or a raindrop strikes the fungus, spores (seeds) are puffed out of a hole in the top. In just one day, a giant puffball can release seven billion spores.

Fairy ring

Toadstools spring from underground filaments called a mycelium. Some toadstools appear as if by magic, in a circle overnight, as the mycelium grows out from a central point. These formations are often called "fairy rings."

Petroleum nut

The petroleum nut tree, which grows in Borneo and the Philippines, produces a high-octane oil in its seeds. The seeds of one tree yield 12 gallons (53 liters) a year, which is about 3 teaspoonsful every day. The oil is burned in lamps, and was used by the Japanese during World War II to fuel tanks.

Diesel tree

The copaiba tree, which grows in the Amazon, contains an oil similar to diesel. It can produce 2 gallons (9 liters) of this oil every hour. So one tree could yield 48 gallons (218 liters) of fuel in one day, enough to fill the gas tanks of 5 cars. Diesel trees are now being cultivated in Japan for their oil.

Petroleum plant

Petroleum seed

Rubber tree

When a cut is made in the bark of a rubber tree, a sticky white liquid called latex oozes out. Rubber trees flourish in the warm, moist climates of Malaysia, Indonesia, and Thailand. They produce 15,400 tons of rubber every day.

Oak

Oak trees live to a great age – one in Switzerland is thought to be around 930 years old. A mature oak tree draws 20 gallons (90 liters) of water out of the earth every day. Oak trees are very slow-growing. They only grow 0.055 in (1.4 mm) a day.

Rampant growth

Tropical rain forest grows twice as fast as temperate oakwood. Every acre of warm, wet rain forest produces 165 lb of lush new growth per day (67 lb per acre). Every 2.5 acres of rain forest contains 330 tons of 180 different species of trees, 1.1 tons of plants, 1.1 tons of earthworms, and 18 lb (8 kg) of birds.

Trumpet tree
Saplings of the trumpet tree growing on the rain forest floor shoot up toward the light at a rate of 0.28 in (7 mm) in one day.

Tasmanian cider gum
One of the fastest-growing of all trees, the cider gum (native to Tasmania) can grow 0.16 in (4 mm) every day.

Poplar
A poplar tree grows just over 0.118 in (3 mm) every day.

Bristlecone pine
The bristlecone pine grows very slowly, at a rate of only 0.00035 in (0.009 mm) a day. This tree is very long-lived. One specimen is believed to be 4,600 years old.

Lichens
Lichens are extremely slow growers, growing only 0.0001 in (0.0025 mm) a day.

Sleepy creatures

Some animals sleep almost all day long, and others hardly sleep at all. The amount of sleep an animal needs depends partly on how it feeds. The sleepy koala bear has a low-energy diet of leaves, and snoozes for around 22 hours out of 24. The tiny shrew is a carnivore that has to feed almost constantly to survive, leaving very little time for dozing.

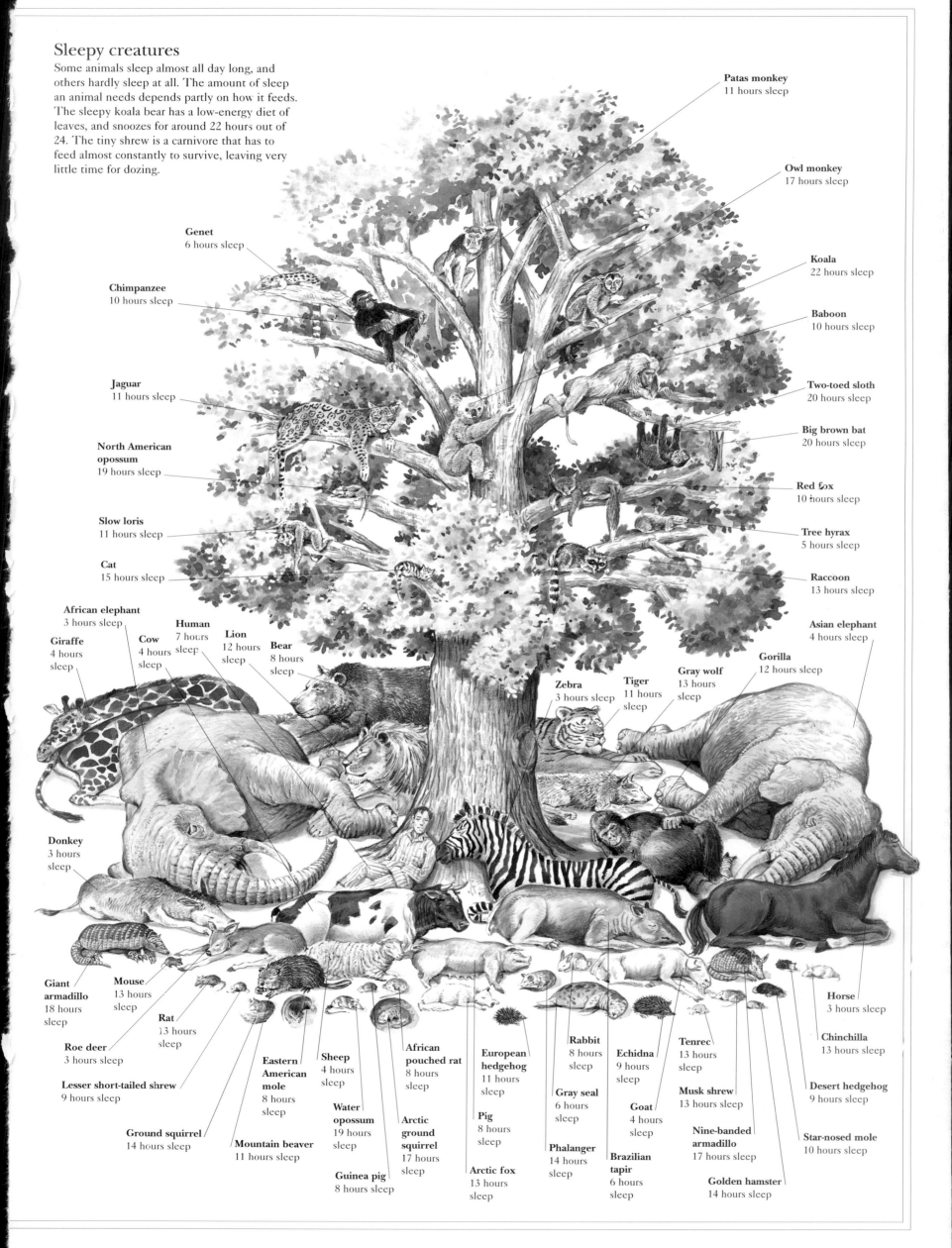

Patas monkey
11 hours sleep

Owl monkey
17 hours sleep

Genet
6 hours sleep

Koala
22 hours sleep

Chimpanzee
10 hours sleep

Baboon
10 hours sleep

Two-toed sloth
20 hours sleep

Jaguar
11 hours sleep

Big brown bat
20 hours sleep

North American opossum
19 hours sleep

Red fox
10 hours sleep

Slow loris
11 hours sleep

Tree hyrax
5 hours sleep

Cat
15 hours sleep

Raccoon
13 hours sleep

African elephant
3 hours sleep

Asian elephant
4 hours sleep

Giraffe
4 hours sleep

Human
7 hours sleep

Cow
4 hours sleep

Lion
12 hours sleep

Bear
8 hours sleep

Gorilla
12 hours sleep

Zebra
3 hours sleep

Tiger
11 hours sleep

Gray wolf
13 hours sleep

Donkey
3 hours sleep

Giant armadillo
18 hours sleep

Mouse
13 hours sleep

Horse
3 hours sleep

Rat
13 hours sleep

Chinchilla
13 hours sleep

Roe deer
3 hours sleep

Rabbit
8 hours sleep

Tenrec
13 hours sleep

Desert hedgehog
9 hours sleep

Lesser short-tailed shrew
9 hours sleep

Eastern American mole
8 hours sleep

Sheep
4 hours sleep

African pouched rat
8 hours sleep

European hedgehog
11 hours sleep

Echidna
9 hours sleep

Musk shrew
13 hours sleep

Gray seal
6 hours sleep

Goat
4 hours sleep

Star-nosed mole
10 hours sleep

Ground squirrel
14 hours sleep

Mountain beaver
11 hours sleep

Water opossum
19 hours sleep

Arctic ground squirrel
17 hours sleep

Pig
8 hours sleep

Phalanger
14 hours sleep

Brazilian tapir
6 hours sleep

Nine-banded armadillo
17 hours sleep

Guinea pig
8 hours sleep

Arctic fox
13 hours sleep

Golden hamster
14 hours sleep

Energetic animals

Some animals have amazing stamina. The rhinoceros beetle can carry 850 times its own weight, while the Arctic tern migrates a distance of over 24,856 miles (40,000 km).

Ostrich
45 mph (72 kph). 1,080 miles (1,728 km) in one day.

Elk
45 mph (72 kph). 1,080 miles (1,728 km) in one day.

Horse
43 mph (70 kph). 1,032 miles (1,680 km) in one day.

Mongolian wild ass
40 mph (64 kph). 960 miles (1,536 km) in one day.

Mole
Moles can dig at a rate of 33 ft (10 m) per hour, so a mole putting in a 24-hour day could dig a tunnel 787 ft (240 m) long.

Chamois
A chamois can climb 13,123 ft (4,000 m) in one hour. In a day it could ascend 10 Mount Everests.

Spider
A spider takes up to an hour to spin a web, so in one day it could spin 24 webs.

Pheasant
37 mph (59 kph). 888 miles (1,416 km) in one day.

Harpy eagle
50 mph (80 kph), diving. 1,200 miles (1,920 km) in one day.

Pigeon
50 mph (80 kph). 1,200 miles (1,920 km) in one day.

Mallard
65 mph (105 kph). 1,560 miles (2,520 km) in one day.

Swift
Flies 621 miles (1,000 km) in one day, when foraging for insects to feed its young.

Wildebeest
50 mph (80 kph). 1,200 miles (1,920 km) in one day.

Eider duck
47 mph (76 kph) 1,128 miles (1,824 km) in one day.

Whooper swan
55 mph (88 kph). 1,320 miles (2,112 km) in one day.

Lion
50 mph (80 kph). 1,200 miles (1,920 km) in one day.

Peregrine falcon
185 mph (298 kph) when diving. 4,440 miles (7,152 km) in one day.

Thomson's gazelle
50 mph (80 kph). 1,200 miles (1,920 km) in one day.

Pronghorn antelope
61 mph (98 kph). 1,464 miles (2,352 km) in one day.

Cheetah
70 mph (113 kph). 2,712 km (1,680 miles) in one day.

ape hunting dog
mph (72 kph).
080 miles (1,728 km)
one day.

Sailfish
68 mph (110 kph). 1,632 miles (2,640 km) in one day.

Flying fish
23 mph (37 kph). 552 miles (888 km) in one day.

Killer whale
35 mph (56 kph). 840 miles (1,344 km) in one day.

Bluefin tuna
46 mph (74 kph). 1,766 km (1,104 miles) in one day.

Marlin
50 mph (80 kph). 1,200 miles (1,920 km) in one day.

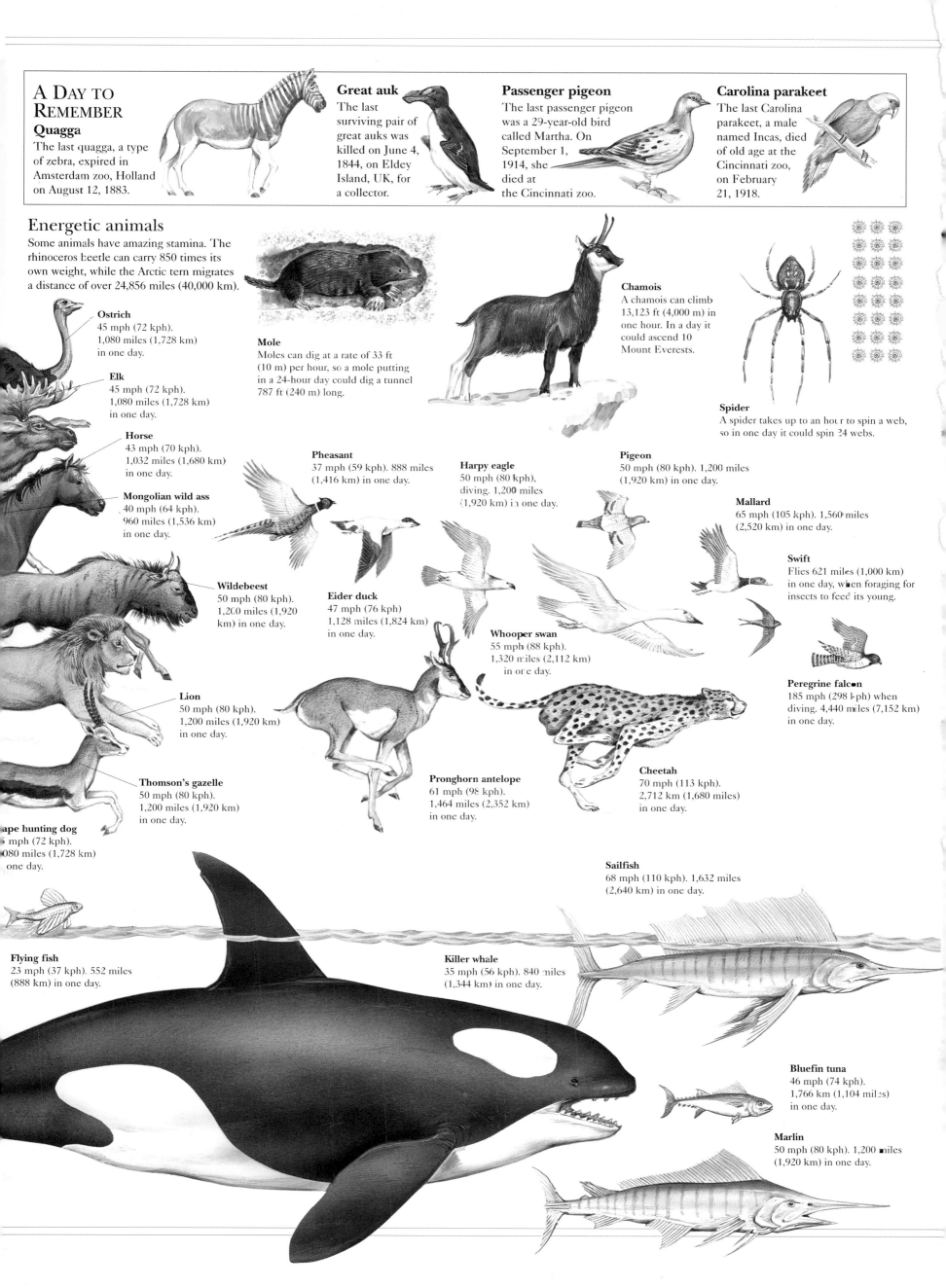

THE HUMAN BODY

EVERY DAY THE HUMAN BODY needs refueling with oxygen, food, and water. The body's powerhouse is the brain. It accounts for only 2 percent of body weight, but uses 20 percent of our oxygen intake, 20 percent of our calorie intake, and 15 percent of the body's blood supply. To fight disease, each body produces 10 billion new white blood cells a day. Skin cells last for 25 days, red blood cells survive for 120 days, liver cells for 500 days, and some nerve cells last a whole lifetime. The continual process of cell renewal that keeps the body alive is called metabolism.

Body factory

The digestive system, lungs, and kidneys are at work around the clock. The digestive system breaks food into particles so tiny that blood can take nourishment to all parts of the body. The body's entire blood supply passes through the lungs almost once a minute, collecting and distributing oxygen. Waste products are removed from the blood in the kidneys, each of which contains around one million tiny filters called nephrons.

Breathtaking stuff

Each one of us takes around 30,000 breaths a day. If you expelled all the air you breathed in a day into rubber dinghies, you would be able to inflate 50 two-man dinghies in 24 hours.

Bloodbath

The average human heart beats 100,800 times a day. The amount of blood that passes through the heart each day would fill 170 bathtubs.

Body heat

The total body heat produced in one day by a human being is enough to power a lightbulb for a day and a half.

House of skin

We shed approximately one million dead skin cells every 40 minutes. One person will shed enough skin in a lifetime to fill a suitcase. All the skin shed by the world's people in one day would fill a four-story house.

Artery

Lungs

Stomach

Large intestine

Small intestine

The average person has around 100,000 hairs growing on his head, and loses and replaces 100 hairs a day.

On average we blink our eyes 9,365 times each day. A single blink lasts 0.15 seconds, so a day's total blinks for one person last 23 minutes. All the world's daily blinks would put us in the dark for 267,000 years.

Human tear production averages about a teaspoonful per day, although crying can spill that much out of the eyes all at once.

A day's beard growth for all the world's men would produce a beard 485 miles (780 km) long. If the daily shaving time of all the world's men were added up, it would produce a shave that lasted 30,000 years.

The human mouth has 3 pairs of salivary glands, which among them produce 2.1 pints (1 liter) of saliva a day.

The kidneys filter impurities from 951 gallons (3,600 liters) of blood every day. That's enough liquid to fill 45 bathtubs.

Food is liquidized in the stomach with the help of acids strong enough to dissolve zinc. It's no wonder that half a million cells lining the stomach die and must be replaced every minute.

It takes about 24 hours for food to travel the full length of the human digestive tract, which is 25 ft (7.5 m) long.

Testis

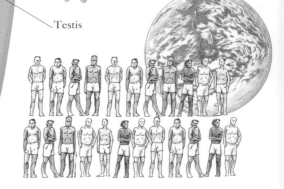

Supersperm

One man's testes produce nearly 300 million sperm cells each day. This means that (in theory!) it would take only 23 men just one day to produce enough sperm to reproduce the entire world population.

Red blood cells are created and destroyed at the rate of 2 million per second. That's 173 billion cells per person per day.

Nails grow at up to 0.004 in (0.1 mm) per day from a bed of active cells under the skin folds at the base and sides of a nail. Fingernails grow up to four times faster than toenails, and both grow faster in warm weather than in cold.

SMALL WORLD

The human body is host to many different kinds of microorganisms, including eyebrow mites and amoebas that swim on our teeth. Around 10 billion bacteria live on the skin and 15 trillion bacteria live in our digestive system.

Fleas can jump 14,400 times a day in search of food, and lay up to 1,000 eggs a day.

A tick can spend a whole day feeding on human blood, and then – after it drops off the skin – a whole year without feeding again.

Tapeworms can live in the small intestine. Every day, hundreds of eggs drop off the worm and are passed in the feces.

The head louse can live on the scalp. It lays up to 10 eggs, called nits, every day. Head lice feed on blood that they suck through the skin.

Mother's milk

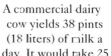

A commercial dairy cow yields 38 pints (18 liters) of milk a day. It would take 25 nursing mothers to produce as much milk in one day as a single commercial dairy cow.

Grand flush

The body produces 3.6 pints (1.7 liters) of urine a day. The total daily world production of human urine would take a full 20 minutes to pass over Niagara Falls. If everyone in the world spent 5 minutes a day in the only bathroom in the world, that bathroom would be occupied for 57,000 years!

It wasn't I!

The human digestive system expels 4.2 pints (2 liters) of gas every day. The average fart is composed of 59% nitrogen, 21% hydrogen, 9% carbon dioxide, 7% methane, and 4% oxygen. That means the world releases enough hydrogen in its daily farts to fill 13 Hindenburg airships.

Around 1,000 brain cells are lost per head per day. But cell loss hardly slows down the nerve impulses of the brain, which travel at around 180 mph (290 kph).

Brainy

During waking hours, the brain constantly perceives and interprets information from the senses, then initiates a response. The brain uses more than 100 billion neurons (nerve cells) every day, and more than 100 trillion synapses (nerve connections) to perform these complex functions.

Sleep tight

While you are awake, you are aware of what you are doing – you are conscious. When you sleep, your conscious brain switches off, but other parts continue the vital task of keeping you alive. In a 24-hour period, the average person spends seven hours asleep. The entire world population spends just over five million years asleep every night!

Transatlantic nails

If all the world's finger- and toenails could be joined together to make one gigantic nail, in just one day it would grow almost from London to New York.

After not cutting his nails for 44 years, the average length of Indian Shindar Chillal's nails was 46 in (117 cm).

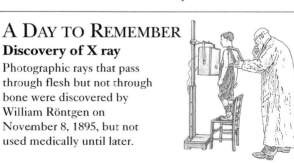

White matter, made up of nerve fibers

Frontal lobe of cerebrum

Cerebellum

Brain stem

You can tell when someone is dreaming by watching their eyelids move. Everyone dreams for about a quarter of their nightly sleep, which means that the total world dream time per night is a million years!

Sweat glands are the body's cooling system. In one day the world's bodies exude enough sweat to fill 16 cargo ships.

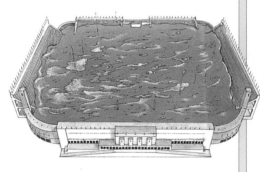

What a stink!

All the human excrement produced in one day would weigh about 1.1 million tons (1 million tonnes). It would fill the enormous Louisiana Superdome, New Orleans, to a depth of 62 ft (9 m).

A male office worker needs to consume 2,400 Cal (10,080 kJ) every day.

A policeman on the beat needs to eat 2,800 Cal (11,760 kJ) every day.

A soldier needs his diet to supply at least 3,500 Cal (14,700 kJ) a day.

Eating for energy

The energy given by the food we eat is measured in calories (Cal) and kilojoules (kJ). Active people need more calories each day than people who sit to work, although the body burns energy even during sleep to keep the metabolism going.

American operating rooms

American operating rooms are the busiest in the world. Around 64,000 operations take place in American hospitals every day. These include 1,540 hysterectomies, 960 bone grafts, 263 hernia operations, 120 cornea grafts, 27 kidney transplants, 15 skin grafts, 9 liver transplants, 6 heart transplants, and 2 lung transplants.

A DAY TO REMEMBER

Discovery of X ray

Photographic rays that pass through flesh but not through bone were discovered by William Röntgen on November 8, 1895, but not used medically until later.

First operation with anesthetic

On March 30, 1842, Dr. Crawford Long of Georgia, removed a cyst from the neck of James M. Venable using ether as an anesthetic.

First vaccination

On May 14, 1796, a British doctor, Dr. Edward Jenner, administered the first vaccination. Eight-year-old James Phipps was vaccinated with cowpox as protection against smallpox.

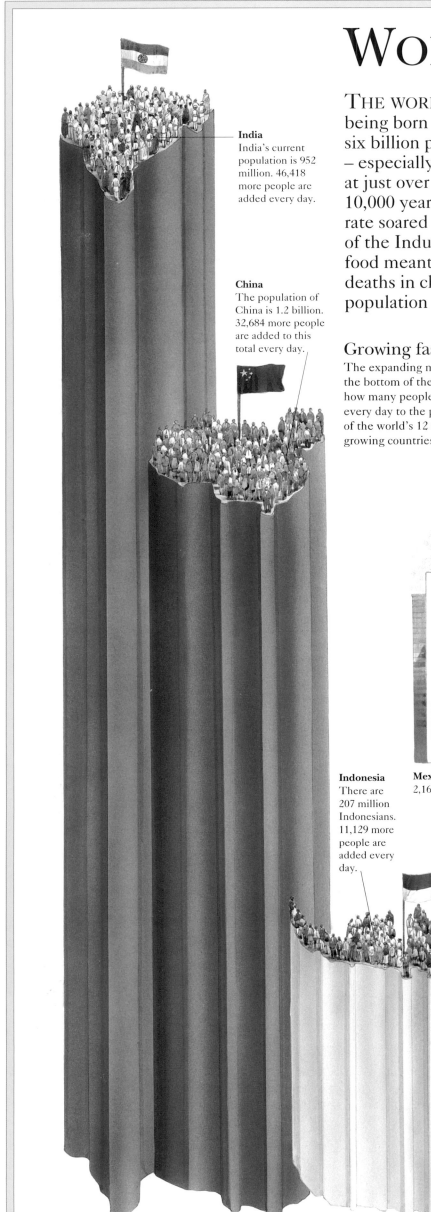

WORLD POPULATION

THE WORLD'S POPULATION IS EXPLODING FAST, with more people being born and living longer than ever before. In 1997, there were almost six billion people on Earth. The human boom is set to continue – especially in Africa, Asia, and Latin America – until, in 2080, it will peak at just over ten billion. The world's population first began to rocket about 10,000 years ago, when people began to grow their own food. The birth rate soared again in the West during the 1800s with the scientific advances of the Industrial Revolution. New methods of growing and transporting food meant that more people ate a better diet. There were also fewer deaths in childhood. Today, 12 times more people are added to the population of the world every day than would have been 100 years ago.

Growing fast
The expanding maps along the bottom of the page show how many people are added every day to the populations of the world's 12 fastest growing countries.

Expanding cities
In many parts of the world, people are moving from rural areas to cities to find work and a better standard of living. Some of the world's largest cities are bursting at the seams, with people living in slums or shanty towns on the outskirts. Mexico City has expanded from nine million people at its heart to 24 million people. Sao Paulo has grown from nine million at the center to 21.5 million, and Seoul from ten million to 19 million.

India
India's current population is 952 million. 46,418 more people are added every day.

China
The population of China is 1.2 billion. 32,684 more people are added to this total every day.

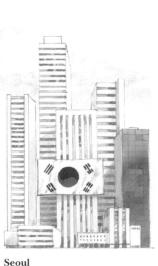

Mexico City
2,169 more people every day

Sao Paulo
2,090 more people every day

Seoul
1,595 more people every day

Indonesia
There are 207 million Indonesians. 11,129 more people are added every day.

Pakistan
Pakistan's population is 129 million. 9,508 more people are added every day.

Nigeria
104 million people live in Nigeria. 8,257 more people are added every day.

US
The population of the US is 266 million. 6,990 more people are added every day.

A DAY TO REMEMBER

Baby in a tube

The first test tube baby was Louise Brown. She was born in Oldham, in the UK, on July 25, 1978.

"We do!"

The largest ever wedding was conducted by Sun Myung Moon in Seoul, Korea, on August 25, 1995. He married 35,000 couples in the Olympic Stadium, and 325,000 other couples around the world by satellite link.

Cold as death

Dr. James Bedford was the first person to be frozen after death, on January 12, 1967, in accordance with the science of cryonics. His body will be defrosted when a cure is found for the illness that killed him.

Dead end

Every day around the world, nearly 150,000 people take their last breath and die. Many die of old age, some perish in accidents or are murdered, while fatal diseases kill the rest.

Heart disease
33,000 die every day.

Diarrhea
14,000 die every day.

Cancer
13,500 die every day.

A whale of a day

The total weight of all the 364,321 babies born in the world in one day is 760 tons (690 tonnes). This is the same weight as five blue whales.

Pneumonia
13,500 die every day.

Tuberculosis
8,200 die every day.

Malaria
5,800 die every day.

Measles
4,000 die every day.

Whooping cough
1,400 die every day.

Happy birthday!

Every day across the world, 16.5 million people celebrate their birthday. In many countries people mark the day with a feast or party. To mark a first birthday in Korea, the child is sat at a table with various objects on it – whichever he or she picks up is said to determine that child's future. Many Buddhists celebrate their birthdays by taking gifts of food to monks, and by releasing fish, turtles, and birds at the temple.

SMALL WORLD

China has more people than any other country on Earth, with a population of 1.2 billion. Overcrowding, and a shortage of resources including food, health care, and education, has caused the Chinese government to restrict family sizes in order to slow population growth rate. Chinese couples are encouraged to postpone marriage until their late 20s. In some areas, parents are allowed to have only one child.

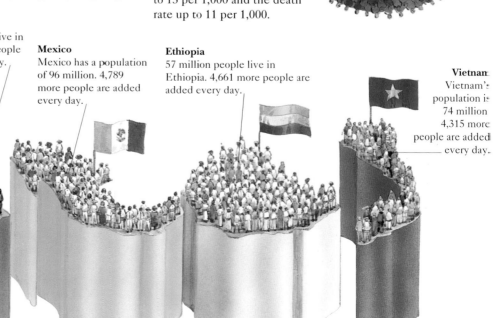

Births and deaths

In one day all over the world, 364,321 people are born and 147,137 people die. So every day there are 217,184 more people on Earth.

Each coffin represents 10,000 deaths.

Each baby in swaddling clothes represents 10,000 births.

Crowded planet

A hundred years from now, 378,000 people will be born every day, and 324,000 people will die. So every day, there will be 54,000 more people on Earth. In 1996 the world birth rate was 25 per 1,000, and the death rate, 9 per 1,000. In 2100, the World Bank predicts that the birth rate will be down to 13 per 1,000 and the death rate up to 11 per 1,000.

Brazil
163 million people live in Brazil. 6,757 more are added every day.

Bangladesh
Bangladesh has a population of 123 million. 6,186 more people are added every day.

Iran
66 million people live in Iran. 4,945 more people are added every day.

Mexico
Mexico has a population of 96 million. 4,789 more people are added every day.

Ethiopia
57 million people live in Ethiopia. 4,661 more people are added every day.

Vietnam
Vietnam's population is 74 million. 4,315 more people are added every day.

ONE DAY'S FOOD

IT WOULD TAKE 75 SUPERTANKERS to carry one day's food for the entire planet. Most people rely on wheat, rice, and corn for their basic food. Adults need about 2,500 calories of food energy a day. However, while Westerners consume up to 4,000 calories a day, some Africans survive on barely 1,800 calories each. And every day, 35,000 people die of starvation. Nutritious vegetables may hold the answer to the world's food needs. A field of soybeans yields 30 times more body-building protein than a field on which beef cattle are raised.

654,000 beef cattle are slaughtered every day.

The world slaughters 2.8 million pigs a day.

1.2 million sheep are slaughtered every day.

Almost 70 million chickens are slaughtered every day worldwide.

Meat
Every day, the world eats 587,500 tons (533,500 tonnes) of meat, the same weight as a herd of a million cows. But if everyone had a share of the world's meat, there would be barely enough for two mouthfuls a day each.

Food city
This is what the world's daily helpings of some of its most nutritious foodstuffs would look like, delivered into the heart of a modern city.

Potatoes
We dig up 801,000 tons (727,000 tonnes) of potatoes every day.

Grapes
The world's grape harvest for one day weighs 171,000 tons (155,000 tonnes) – that's 22 billion individual grapes.

Beans and lentils
In one day, the world produces 177,000 tons (161,000 tonnes) of beans and lentils.

Bananas
The world's daily banana harvest is 159,000 tons (144,000 tonnes).

Cabbages
The world produces 121,000 tons (110,000 tonnes) of cabbages in a day.

Watermelons
Every day 88,000 tons (80,000 tonnes) of watermelons are harvested.

Cocoa
The world produces 7,700 tons (7,000 tonnes) of cocoa beans every day. That's enough to make 600 million bars of chocolate.

Peas
Every day, the world harvests 13,200 tons (12,000 tonnes) of peas. That's enough to give 300 million people a serving of peas.

The fastest food in the world
Every day, Americans munch through 7 million pizzas, 4,400 tons (4,000 tonnes) of potato chips, 440 tons (400 tonnes) of pretzels, 300,000 cans of Spam, around 15 million burgers, 4 million gallons of ice cream, 250 million sodas, as well as 5 French fries each.

Tea
Worldwide 7,700 tons (7,000 tonnes) of tea leaves are produced every day. That's enough for 3 billion cups of tea.

Cucumbers
The world grows 58,000 tons (53,000 tonnes) of cucumbers every day. That's enough for everyone in India and China to have a cucumber sandwich.

Onions
The world's daily onion harvest weighs 98,000 tons (89,000 tonnes), as much as the ocean liner *Queen Elizabeth*.

Salt
The world harvests 551,000 tons (500,000 tonnes) of salt in a day.

Fries
Soda
Burgers
Ice cream
Pretzels
Pizza

Eggs
Eggs are a complete food because they provide all the proteins the body needs for tissue growth and repair. Today China is the world's biggest egg-producing nation. The world's hen population lays nearly 2 billion eggs a day, which would make an omelette as big as the island of Cyprus.

Japan
The Japanese eat 27,500 tons (25,000 tonnes) of fish a day.

France
The French love the pungent flavor of garlic. France produces 150,000 tons (145 tonnes) of garlic every day.

China
The Chinese lead the world in rice production. They eat rice at every meal, getting through 402,000 tons (365,000 tonnes) every day.

Greece
The Greeks eat more bread than anyone else in the world – 9 oz (300 g) per person per day.

Wheat
Wheat is one of the world's major food crops, with 1.5 million tons (1.4 million tonnes) harvested every day. The world eats enough wheat in one day to make a loaf as heavy as three Empire State Buildings.

Rice
Nearly 1.6 million tons (1.5 million tonnes) of rice is harvested every day and about half of the world's population eats it as the main ingredient of meals. The world's daily helping of rice would make a heap six times as big as Egypt's Great Pyramid.

Tomatoes
All the tomatoes eaten in the world in one day weigh 234,000 tons (212,000 tonnes).

Corn
Every day 1.8 million tons (1.6 million tonnes) of corn is harvested, and the world eats enough corn to equal the weight of 300,000 African elephants.

Oranges
The orange is probably the world's most popular fruit – 176,000 tons (160,000 tonnes) are picked every day.

Pineapples
The world produces 35,900 tons (32,000 tonnes) of pineapples every day.

Sugar
The world produces 148,000 tons (134,000 tonnes) of sugar a day

Apples
The world's daily apple harvest is 148,000 tons (134,000 tonnes).

Lemons and limes
In one day, the world produces 23,000 tons (21,000 tonnes) of lemons and limes.

Garlic
Every day 24,000 tons (22,000 tonnes) of garlic are produced worldwide.

Apricots
The world's daily apricot harvest weighs 6,600 tons (6,000 tonnes) and would fill 6 barges.

Avocados
The world avocado harvest weighs in at 5,500 tons (5,000 tonnes) a day.

Pumpkins
The world produces 25,000 tons (23,000 tonnes) of pumpkins in a day.

Mangoes
In one day the world produces 56,000 tons (51,000 tonnes) of mangos.

Strawberries
The world's daily consumption of strawberries is 6,600 tons (6,000 tonnes).

Raspberries
The world produces enough raspberries every day to fill a train pulling 23 cars.

Carrots
In one day the world produces 43,000 tons (39,000 tonnes) of carrots.

Coconuts
In a day the world produces 133,000 tons (121,000 tonnes) of coconuts.

Caviar
The world produces 3 tons (2.7 tonnes) of caviar in a day.

High-flying food
Nearly 3 million meals are served in the air every day.

Honey
In one day bees sip the nectar from 3 trillion flowers. They make 3,300 tons (3,000 tonnes) of honey, enough to cover a slice of toast as big as London.

OUT OF THIS WORLD
The first astronauts ate cold paste that they squeezed from a tube. Today's astronauts have a menu of more than 70 items. Some of these are in cans or foil bags. Others need to have water added. Many are heated before eating. Astronauts eat from trays strapped to their laps.

PRODUCTION

THE WORLD IS A MIGHTY PRODUCTION machine, every day its factories and offices churn out billions of dollars worth of "stuff." It's strange to think that machines were invented less than 300 years ago, and before that time, everything was made at home, by hand. The first machines were powered by renewable energy – the sweat of human effort, and water turning a wheel. But the age of steam was fired by coal, so the first really efficient machines began to gobble up Earth's natural resources. Today the world uses the equivalent of 8 lb (4 kg) of oil per person a day – though Americans consume 5½ times that amount!

What a gas!
Every day, world natural gas production is nearly 212 billion cu ft (6 billion cu m). One day's gas for the whole world would fill 2.6 million hot-air balloons.

Coal
The world produces 13 million tons (12 million tonnes) of coal a day. This creates a daily heap of coal as tall as the Eiffel Tower.

Hoover Dam

Cement
The world produces 3.5 million tons (3.2 million tonnes) of cement in a day. This would make 17 million tons (16 million tonnes) of concrete – enough to build 3 Hoover Dams.

Jewel in the crown
274,000 karats of diamonds are mined every day. A karat is 0.02 g, so the world's daily output of diamonds is less than 12 lb (5.5 kg).

Dam powerful
The world's hydroelectric dams produce 2.4 billion kw of electricity every day. So, each day, they save the world from burning 500,000 tons (600,000 tonnes) of oil. One day's hydroelectricity for the world could power a 100W lightbulb for a billion days – 2.7 million years.

Black gold
The world produces almost 9.92 million tons (9 million tonnes) of oil a day, which is enough to fill the holds of 90 cargo ships. Every day in the world's refineries, 2.5 million tons (2.3 million tonnes) of oil is turned into gas, and 1.5 million tons (1.4 million tonnes) is used to manufacture plastics.

Crude wealth
A typical oil rig can pump up 189,000 barrels of precious crude oil from the Earth every day.

Neon city
A nuclear power station could produce enough electricity in a day to supply the city of Las Vegas for 8 years.

Cars, cars, cars
Every day, a staggering 137,000 vehicles roll off the world's production lines. The US is the world's biggest car manufacturer, but the people of Luxembourg own more cars per head than any other nation in the world. In Luxembourg there are 57 cars on the road for every 100 people.

US
The US produces 32,836 vehicles a day.

Japan
Japan manufactures 27,933 vehicles every day.

France
The French manufacture 9,520 vehicles daily.

Germany
12,787 vehicles roll off Germany's production lines each day.

South Korea
In South Korea, 6,922 vehicles are produced every day.

Canada
Every day Canada's factories produce over 6,662 vehicles.

Spain
Spain manufactures 6,394 vehicles a day.

UK
4,836 vehicles roll out of the assembly plant every day in the UK.

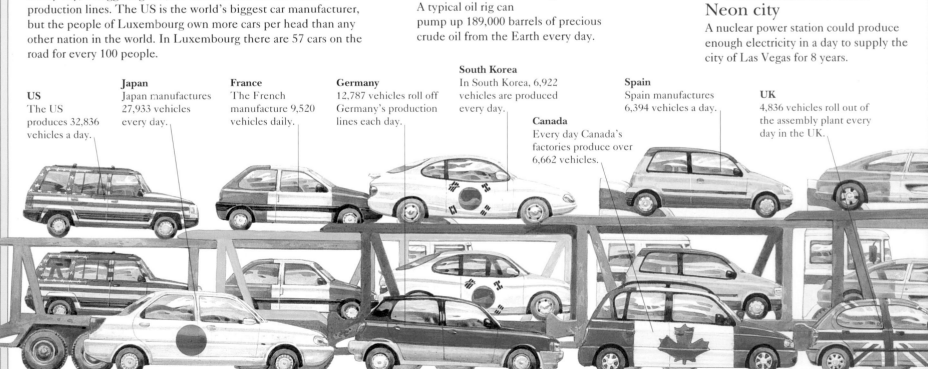

Awesome ores

Metals are extracted from ores – naturally occurring minerals that are mined from the Earth.

The world produces 33,000 tons (30,000 tonnes) of copper every day. That would make enough copper piping to encircle the globe 3 times.

600,000 tons (555,000 tonnes) of aluminum are produced in a day, enough to make more than 17 billion soda cans.

The world's mines yield 110 tons (100 tonnes) of uranium every day. Uranium is used to power nuclear reactors.

Daily world production of platinum is 176 lb (80 kg). It is used in electrical instruments and jewelry.

The world output of mercury is 9 tons (8 tonnes) a day, enough to fill nearly 7 million thermometers.

MONEY WORLD

The world's banks send money to each other 24 hours a day. Instead of cash, they transmit computer messages giving the amount. In one day, banks exchange over 1.5 million electronic messages. In this way, about $2 trillion moves around the globe every day. As well as money itself, the global financial markets trade in stocks and bonds, which may be shares in business companies. The total value of the world's tradable stocks and bonds is $8.5 trillion.

"This pile of timber was built in one day, and it reaches up into space – or so they tell me!"

Great heaps of stuff

If all the tons of different stuff produced in the world in a single day could be piled up into heaps, the landscape would be dominated by mountains of useful goods. The daily powdered laundry detergent pile would be big enough to ski down, and one day's timber pile would reach up into outer space.

Timber
Worldwide, enough timber is cut every day to produce 150 million planks of wood. If all the logs cut in a day were used to build a tower, it would reach up into outer space.

Steel
Around 3.3 million tons (2 million tonnes) of steel is produced every day. If all this steel was turned into cars, it would make 2.5 million vehicles in one day.

Computers
IBM manufactures 20,000 computers a day.

Soap powder
59,000 tons (54,000 tonnes) of soap and laundry detergent are produced in a day. That would be enough to wash 2 loads of laundry for each US citizen.

"I'll sleep like a log after building this tower!"

Gold rush

7 tons (6.3 tonnes) of gold is mined in one day – more than a quarter of it comes from South Africa. Gold is so dense that the world's daily gold extraction could fit inside a refrigerator. Every day, 330 lb (150 kg) of gold (much of it recycled) is used to fill teeth – that's the weight of more than 2 adults.

Washing machines
The world churns out 101,000 washing machines a day.

A new car every day

The number of cars in the world is increasing at a little more than half the rate of world population growth. Every day, at least one new car is produced for every other additional person on the planet.

Tires
2.3 million tires are manufactured every day, almost a quarter of them in the US.

Refrigerators
Worldwide, 137,000 refrigerators are made every day.

String
If you made the world's daily harvest of around 11,000 tons (10,000 tonnes) of jute, sisal, and hemp into string, it would be 4 million miles (6.5 million km) long. It would stretch 17 times from the Earth to the Moon.

"This is the cleanest ski slope I've ever seen!"

Italy
4,568 vehicles are manufactured in Italy every day.

Brazil
Brazil produces 3,737 vehicles daily.

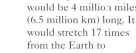

WASTE AND RECYCLING

RECYCLING GARBAGE MEANS that we take fewer raw materials from the Earth. Recycling paper the world over eliminates the need to cut down five million trees every day. Recycling also helps to save energy. With the amount of energy needed to make one aluminum can from raw materials, 20 can be made from recycled aluminum. Most household waste can be recycled. Kitchen scraps can be composted, and glass taken to a bottle bank to be crushed and melted down to make new glass. Plastics can be shredded, melted, and reformed.

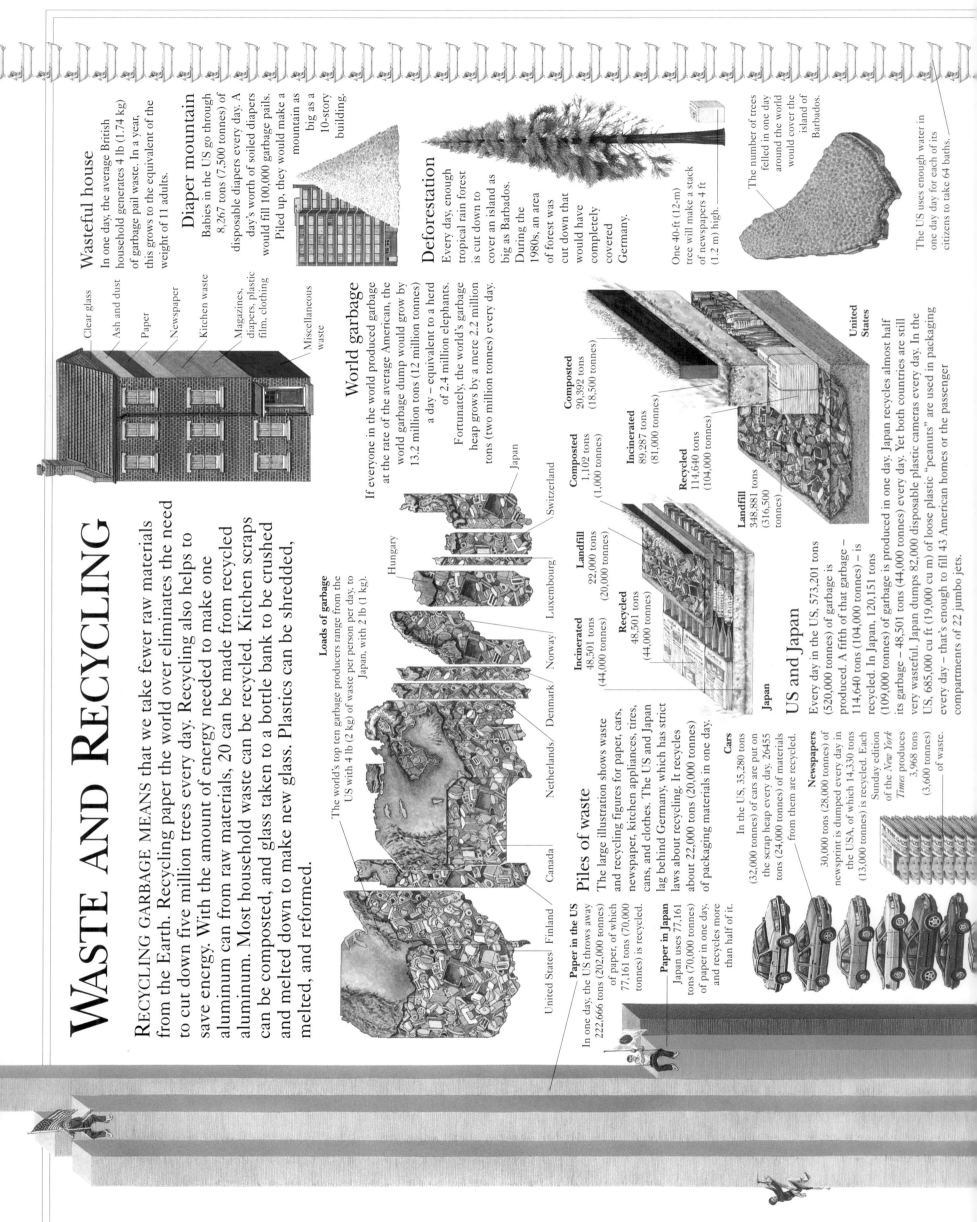

Wasteful house

In one day, the average British household generates 4 lb (1.74 kg) of garbage pail waste. In a year, this grows to the equivalent of the weight of 11 adults.

Clear glass
Ash and dust
Paper
Newspaper
Kitchen waste
Magazines, diapers, plastic film, clothing
Miscellaneous waste

Diaper mountain

Babies in the US go through 8,267 tons (7,500 tonnes) of disposable diapers every day. A day's worth of soiled diapers would fill 100,000 garbage pails. Piled up, they would make a mountain as big as a 10-story building.

Deforestation

Every day, enough tropical rain forest is cut down to cover an island as big as Barbados. During the 1980s, an area of forest was cut down that would have completely covered Germany.

One 40-ft (12-m) tree will make a stack of newspapers 4 ft (1.2 m) high.

The number of trees felled in one day around the world would cover the island of Barbados.

The US uses enough water in one day for each of its citizens to take 64 baths.

World garbage

If everyone in the world produced garbage at the rate of the average American, the world garbage dump would grow by 13.2 million tons (12 million tonnes) a day – equivalent to a herd of 2.4 million elephants. Fortunately, the world's garbage heap grows by a mere 2.2 million tons (two million tonnes) every day.

Japan
Switzerland
Hungary
Luxembourg
Norway
Denmark
Netherlands
Canada
Finland
United States

Loads of garbage

The world's top ten garbage producers range from the US with 4 lb (2 kg) of waste per person per day, to Japan, with 2 lb (1 kg).

Piles of waste

The large illustration shows waste and recycling figures for paper, cars, newspaper, kitchen appliances, tires, cans, and clothes. The US and Japan lag behind Germany, which has strict laws about recycling. It recycles about 22,000 tons (20,000 tonnes) of packaging materials in one day.

Paper in the US
In one day, the US throws away 222,666 tons (202,000 tonnes) of paper, of which 77,161 tons (70,000 tonnes) is recycled.

Paper in Japan
Japan uses 77,161 tons (70,000 tonnes) of paper in one day, and recycles more than half of it.

Cars
In the US, 35,280 tons (32,000 tonnes) of cars are put on the scrap heap every day. 26455 tons (24,000 tonnes) of materials from them are recycled.

Newspapers
30,000 tons (28,000 tonnes) of newsprint is dumped every day in the USA, of which 14,330 tons (13,000 tonnes) is recycled. Each Sunday edition of the New York Times produces 3,968 tons (3,600 tonnes) of waste.

United States
Composted 20,392 tons (18,500 tonnes)
Incinerated 89,287 tons (81,000 tonnes)
Recycled 114,640 tons (104,000 tonnes)
Landfill 348,881 tons (316,500 tonnes)

Japan
Composted 1,102 tons (1,000 tonnes)
Incinerated 48,501 tons (44,000 tonnes)
Recycled 48,501 tons (44,000 tonnes)
Landfill 22,000 tons (20,000 tonnes)

US and Japan

Every day in the US, 573,201 tons (520,000 tonnes) of garbage is produced. A fifth of that garbage – 114,640 tons (104,000 tonnes) – is recycled. In Japan, 120,151 tons (109,000 tonnes) of garbage is produced in one day. Japan recycles almost half its garbage – 48,501 tons (44,000 tonnes) every day. Yet both countries are still very wasteful. Japan dumps 82,000 disposable plastic cameras every day. In the US, 685,000 cu ft (19,000 cu m) of loose plastic "peanuts" are used in packaging every day – that's enough to fill 43 American homes or the passenger compartments of 22 jumbo jets.

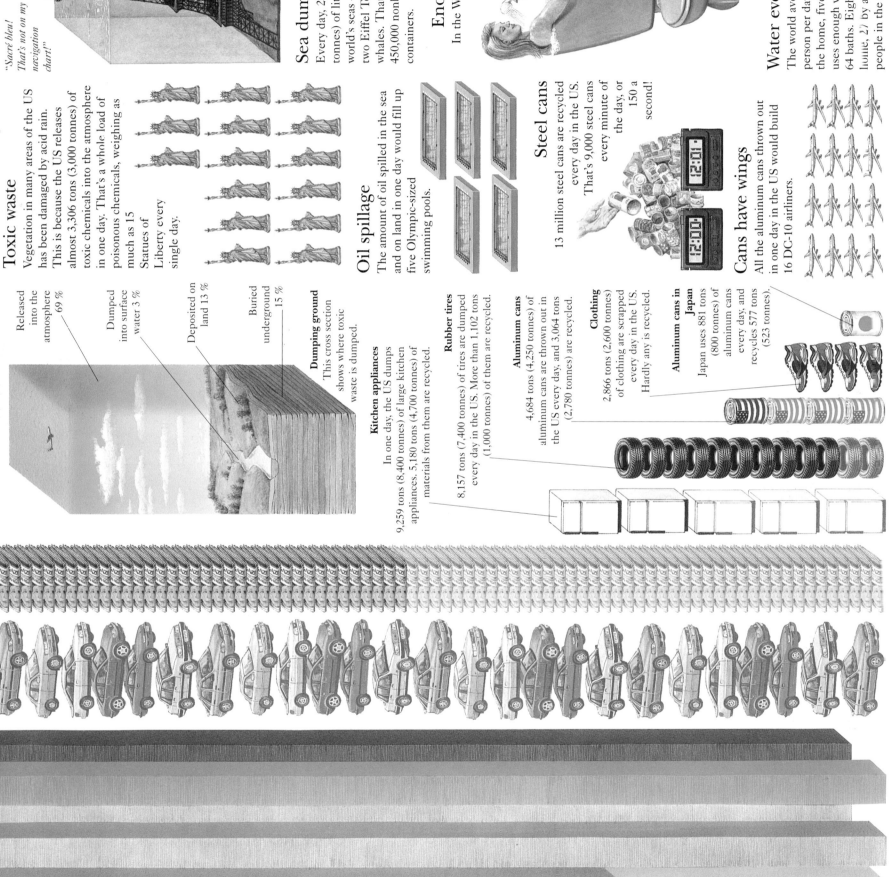

The world average consumption of water is one third that of the US.

Toxic waste

Vegetation in many areas of the US has been damaged by acid rain. This is because the US releases almost 3,306 tons (3,000 tonnes) of toxic chemicals into the atmosphere in one day. That's a whole load of poisonous chemicals, weighing as much as 15 Statues of Liberty every single day.

"Sacré bleu! That's not on my navigation chart!"

Sea dumping

Every day, 20,000 tons (18,000 tonnes) of litter is chucked into the world's seas – the same weight as two Eiffel Towers or 136 blue whales. That garbage includes 450,000 nonbiodegradable plastic containers.

Enough for a bath

In the Western world, everyone uses about 30 gallons (135 liters) of water every day just to flush the toilet. That's enough for one and a half baths.

"I'm flushing away all my worries!"

Water everywhere

The world average consumption of water is 22 bathfuls per person per day. For each person, two bathfuls are used in the home, five by industry, and 15 by agriculture. The US uses enough water every day for each of its citizens to take 64 baths. Eight bathfuls of water per person are used in the home, 2⅓ by agriculture, and 29 by industry. Yet 1.2 billion people in the developing world lack safe drinking water.

Oil spillage

The amount of oil spilled in the sea and on land in one day would fill up five Olympic-sized swimming pools.

Steel cans

13 million steel cans are recycled every day in the US. That's 9,000 steel cans every minute of the day, or 150 a second!

Cans have wings

All the aluminum cans thrown out in one day in the US would build 16 DC-10 airliners.

Released into the atmosphere 69 %

Dumped into surface water 3 %

Deposited on land 13 %

Buried underground 15 %

Dumping ground
This cross section shows where toxic waste is dumped.

Kitchen appliances
In one day, the US dumps 9,259 tons (8,400 tonnes) of large kitchen appliances. 5,180 tons (4,700 tonnes) of materials from them are recycled.

Rubber tires
8,157 tons (7,400 tonnes) of tires are dumped every day in the US. More than 1,102 tons (1,000 tonnes) of them are recycled.

Aluminum cans
4,684 tons (4,250 tonnes) of aluminum cans are thrown out in the US every day, and 3,064 tons (2,780 tonnes) are recycled.

Clothing
2,866 tons (2,600 tonnes) of clothing are scrapped every day in the US. Hardly any is recycled.

Aluminum cans in Japan
Japan uses 881 tons (800 tonnes) of aluminum cans every day, and recycles 577 tons (523 tonnes).

COMMUNICATIONS

WORDS WERE FIRST SPOKEN by human mouths into human ears around 40,000 years ago. Today words can reach destinations on the other side of the globe almost as soon as they are uttered. Radio signals are bounced back to receiving stations by Earth's atmosphere, and satellites in space allow people to talk to each other, face to face, day and night, all across the planet. Our voices have escaped into space in the form of radio waves, and our first words have passed within 70 light-years of the Sun. We have also beamed out messages, hoping to get in touch with alien beings – but as yet, no signal has been received from other worlds.

How satellite communications work

High-frequency signals for telephone, computer, and television pass straight through Earth's atmosphere. They need satellites in space to bounce them back to Earth. The higher the satellite, the greater the area of Earth it can cover.

UOSAT 12
Each day, University of Surrey Satellite 12 travels around the Earth 16 times. It is testing a propulsion system that uses steam instead of poisonous gas.

OPTUS B
Optus B travels 540,000 miles (864,000 km) each day, providing Australia and the Pacific with telephone and broadcasting links.

European weather satellite

Defense Support Program
DSP is a US missile-warning satellite. Its infrared sensors can detect hot exhaust from a nuclear missile. It scans the surface of the Earth at 6 revolutions per minute, which is 8,640 times a day.

SOHO
Every day, SOHO (Solar and Heliospheric Observatory) measures millions of sunquakes or vibrations on the surface of the Sun.

Iridium
This is one of a series of 66 low-Earth orbit communications satellites launched in 1997. Each day, Iridium can transfer thousands of calls from mobile phones.

Infrared Space Observatory
Each day, the tank of supercold helium in ISO cools instruments to –455.8°F (–271°C), and allows them to measure tiny amounts of heat arriving from planets, gas clouds, and galaxies.

Molniya
Molniya provides communications coverage (television and telephone calls) for the most northerly regions of Russia for about 8 hours every day.

Space Shuttle
In one day, the space shuttle can carry a crew of seven astronauts around the world 16 times, while they service and repair other craft, carry out scientific experiments, or take hundreds of photos of Earth.

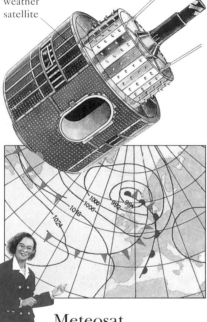

Meteosat

This Meteosat craft hovers over the Atlantic Ocean, from where it can "see" Europe's weather coming. Every day, it observes cloud movement, so weather forecasters can predict the weather for several days ahead.

Is anyone out there?

Radio telescopes on Earth are listening day and night for messages from space, but after almost 40 years, not one has been picked up! In 1974 we sent a message to a distant star cluster from Arecibo Observatory, Puerto Rico, the world's biggest radio telescope. It will be the 270th century before it gets there, and the 520th century before we could receive a reply!

"Sorry, wrong galaxy!"

Pioneer 10

The space probe Pioneer 10 was the first spacecraft to cross the asteroid belt and fly past Jupiter. It is now 9.7 billion miles (15.6 billion km) from Earth. Every day it travels 334,000 miles (536,000 km) into space.

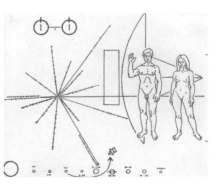

Message to other worlds

On its side, Pioneer 10 carries a plaque showing human figures and a diagram of the Earth's position in the universe. It is hoped that one day aliens will find the craft and communicate with Earth.

Letters from America

US
The US handles 603 million pieces of mail in one day.

The world sends 1.2 billion letters through the mail every day. If all these letters could be stacked together, they would make a bridge that would span the Atlantic Ocean.

UK
The UK handles around 50 million pieces of mail a day – that's one letter every day for each of the inhabitants of the British Isles.

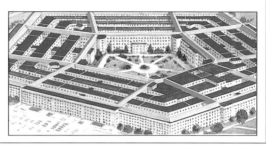

SMALL WORLD

The Pentagon, Arlington, Virginia, is the headquarters of the American Department of Defense. It has one of the world's largest private telephone systems, with 34,500 individual lines, handling a million calls a day. It also has the world's largest pneumatic tube system, with 15 miles (24 km) of tube, through which letters are transported by means of air pressure.

HALCA
This Japanese radio astronomy satellite travels around Earth 4 times every day.

With love from me to you

Christmas Day is celebrated in the US with 2.7 billion festive cards. And one million romantic Americans lick stamps each year to make the mail for Valentine's Day on February 14.

INTELSAT 8
Each day, Intelsats are able to relay up to 112,500 two-way telephone conversations at the same time, as well as 3 television channels.

Stampede

Americans lick about 13.7 million stamps every day. Pasted edge to edge, they would cover 2 American football fields.

"I know a secret, but my lips are sealed!"

"I'm out of the country right now."

'Allo? 'Allo?

Every day, 652 million telephone lines and more than 100 million mobile phones are in use across the world. Most of the talking goes on in North America. The average American makes 5 calls a day. If the total daily calls between the US and Canada were added up into a single conversation, they would make a telephone call that lasted 23 years!

"Your Shuttle needs a tune-up, buddy."

NAVSTAR
NAVSTAR is a series of 24 navigation satellites. Each satellite travels around the Earth twice a day, sending signals that help boats and planes locate their positions.

ACTS
The Advanced Communications Technology Satellite takes exactly 24 hours to orbit the Earth as it spins on its axis.

"Salut!"

"Hello!"

"Bore da!"

"Jambo!"

"Iska warran!"

"Hej!"

"Ciao!"

Computer-speak

Computers were first used for communications in 1969 by scientists and academics. Now, people in 150 countries around the globe talk to each other every day on the Internet.

"Dumela!"

Let's chat

Every day, people around the world communicate with each other in thousands of different languages, each with its own culture and tradition.

"Hoi!"

Hubble Space Telescope
Each day, HST takes pictures of planets, stars, dust clouds, black holes, and quasars. With new cameras fitted in 1997, HST can see far back into the past, detecting the first galaxies soon after they were born.

"Alo!"

"Kumusta!"

Don't shoot the messenger

Every business day, Federal Express delivers more than 2 million items to over 200 countries around the world.

Flower power

Every day, the British communicate happiness, sympathy, or regret by sending 11,000 bunches of flowers.

"Bloomin' bootiful!"

A DAY TO REMEMBER

Dots and dashes

On January 8, 1838, the first Morse Code message was sent by a student of Samuel Morse. It read: "A patient waiter is no loser."

Altitude problem

The ballpoint pen was patented on June 10, 1943, by László Josef Biró. It was used by navigators, because fountain pens leak at altitude, and pencils do not mark weatherproof maps.

Royal cable

On August 16, 1858, Queen Victoria sent a formal greeting to American President James Buchanan. She was the first head of state to use the world's first transatlantic cable.

TRAVEL

IF ALL THE FOOTSTEPS TAKEN IN THE WORLD in one day could be put together to make one long journey, the human race could walk 88 times to the Sun and back every 24 hours. On wheels, wings, water, and on foot, this restless world is constantly on the move. Traveling is more comfortable for some than for others. In the West, there is a car for every two people. In Ethiopia, there is only one car for every 1,468 people.

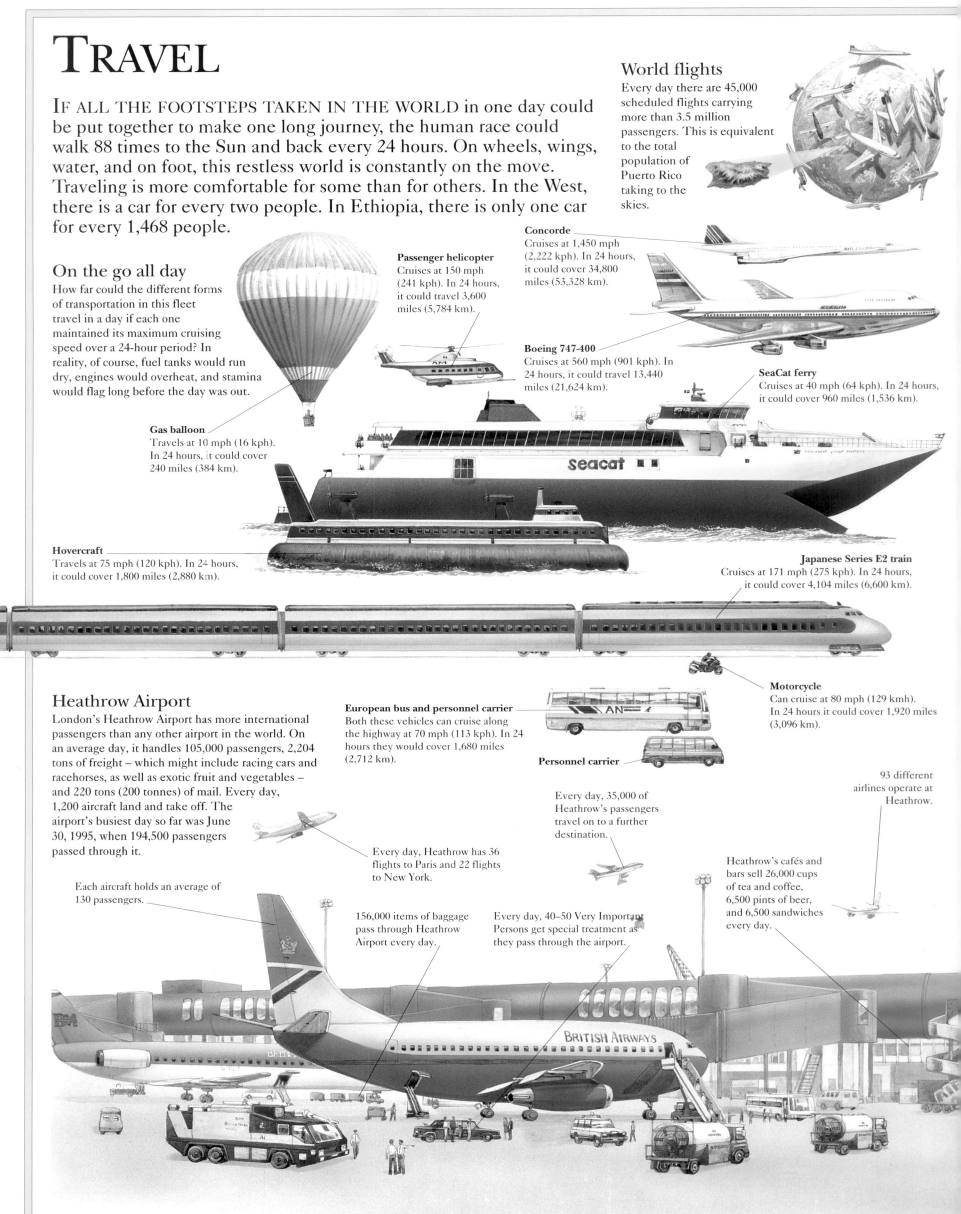

World flights
Every day there are 45,000 scheduled flights carrying more than 3.5 million passengers. This is equivalent to the total population of Puerto Rico taking to the skies.

On the go all day
How far could the different forms of transportation in this fleet travel in a day if each one maintained its maximum cruising speed over a 24-hour period? In reality, of course, fuel tanks would run dry, engines would overheat, and stamina would flag long before the day was out.

Passenger helicopter
Cruises at 150 mph (241 kph). In 24 hours, it could travel 3,600 miles (5,784 km).

Concorde
Cruises at 1,450 mph (2,222 kph). In 24 hours, it could cover 34,800 miles (53,328 km).

Boeing 747-400
Cruises at 560 mph (901 kph). In 24 hours, it could travel 13,440 miles (21,624 km).

SeaCat ferry
Cruises at 40 mph (64 kph). In 24 hours, it could cover 960 miles (1,536 km).

Gas balloon
Travels at 10 mph (16 kph). In 24 hours, it could cover 240 miles (384 km).

Hovercraft
Travels at 75 mph (120 kph). In 24 hours, it could cover 1,800 miles (2,880 km).

Japanese Series E2 train
Cruises at 171 mph (275 kph). In 24 hours, it could cover 4,104 miles (6,600 km).

Motorcycle
Can cruise at 80 mph (129 kmh). In 24 hours it could cover 1,920 miles (3,096 km).

Heathrow Airport
London's Heathrow Airport has more international passengers than any other airport in the world. On an average day, it handles 105,000 passengers, 2,204 tons of freight – which might include racing cars and racehorses, as well as exotic fruit and vegetables – and 220 tons (200 tonnes) of mail. Every day, 1,200 aircraft land and take off. The airport's busiest day so far was June 30, 1995, when 194,500 passengers passed through it.

European bus and personnel carrier
Both these vehicles can cruise along the highway at 70 mph (113 kph). In 24 hours they would cover 1,680 miles (2,712 km).

Personnel carrier

Every day, 35,000 of Heathrow's passengers travel on to a further destination.

93 different airlines operate at Heathrow.

Each aircraft holds an average of 130 passengers.

Every day, Heathrow has 36 flights to Paris and 22 flights to New York.

156,000 items of baggage pass through Heathrow Airport every day.

Every day, 40–50 Very Important Persons get special treatment as they pass through the airport.

Heathrow's cafés and bars sell 26,000 cups of tea and coffee, 6,500 pints of beer, and 6,500 sandwiches every day.

BRITISH AIRWAYS

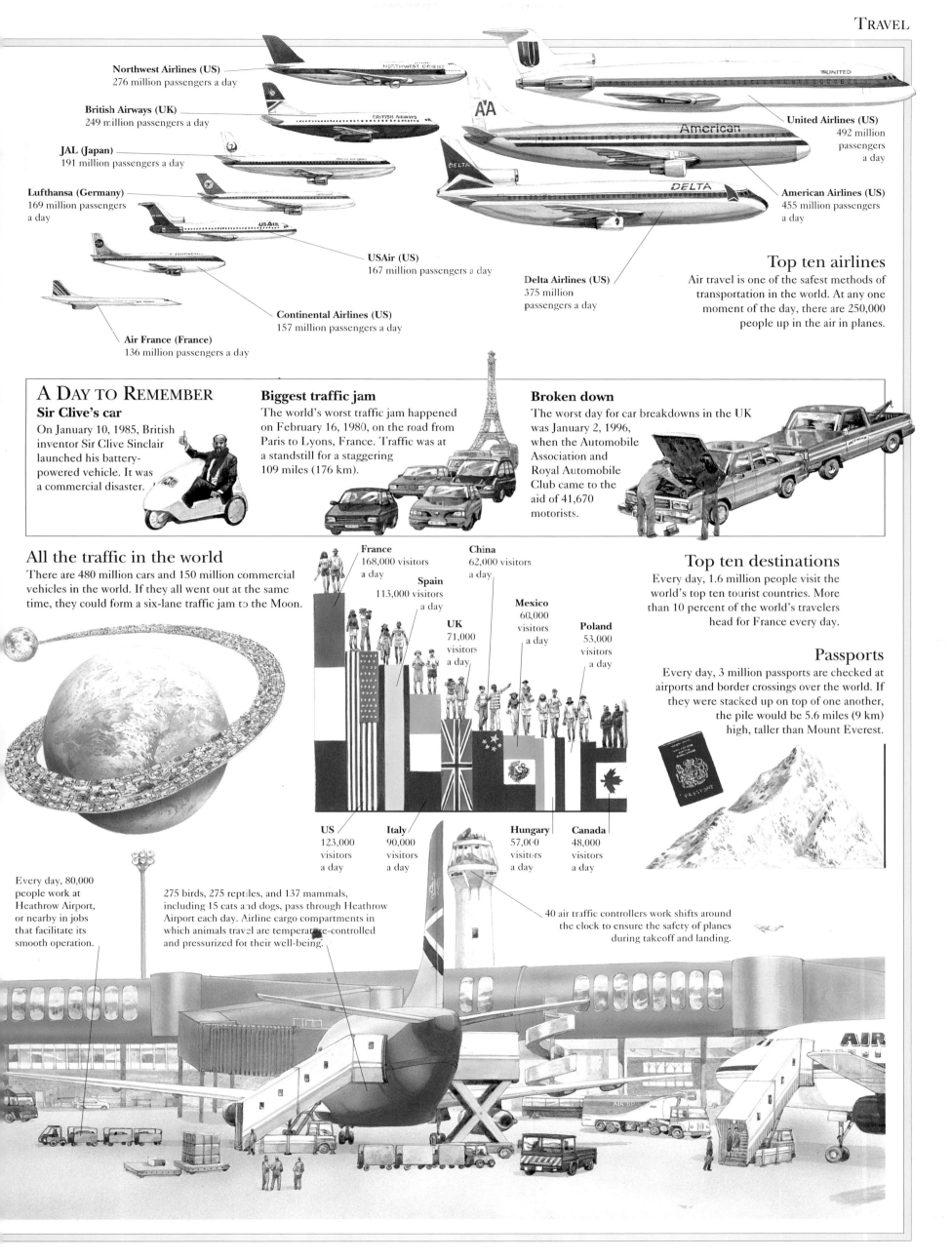

Northwest Airlines (US)
276 million passengers a day

British Airways (UK)
249 million passengers a day

JAL (Japan)
191 million passengers a day

Lufthansa (Germany)
169 million passengers a day

United Airlines (US)
492 million passengers a day

American Airlines (US)
455 million passengers a day

USAir (US)
167 million passengers a day

Delta Airlines (US)
375 million passengers a day

Continental Airlines (US)
157 million passengers a day

Air France (France)
136 million passengers a day

Top ten airlines

Air travel is one of the safest methods of transportation in the world. At any one moment of the day, there are 250,000 people up in the air in planes.

A DAY TO REMEMBER
Sir Clive's car
On January 10, 1985, British inventor Sir Clive Sinclair launched his battery-powered vehicle. It was a commercial disaster.

Biggest traffic jam
The world's worst traffic jam happened on February 16, 1980, on the road from Paris to Lyons, France. Traffic was at a standstill for a staggering 109 miles (176 km).

Broken down
The worst day for car breakdowns in the UK was January 2, 1996, when the Automobile Association and Royal Automobile Club came to the aid of 41,670 motorists.

All the traffic in the world
There are 480 million cars and 150 million commercial vehicles in the world. If they all went out at the same time, they could form a six-lane traffic jam to the Moon.

France
168,000 visitors a day

Spain
113,000 visitors a day

China
62,000 visitors a day

UK
71,000 visitors a day

Mexico
60,000 visitors a day

Poland
53,000 visitors a day

US
123,000 visitors a day

Italy
90,000 visitors a day

Hungary
57,000 visitors a day

Canada
48,000 visitors a day

Top ten destinations
Every day, 1.6 million people visit the world's top ten tourist countries. More than 10 percent of the world's travelers head for France every day.

Passports
Every day, 3 million passports are checked at airports and border crossings over the world. If they were stacked up on top of one another, the pile would be 5.6 miles (9 km) high, taller than Mount Everest.

Every day, 80,000 people work at Heathrow Airport, or nearby in jobs that facilitate its smooth operation.

275 birds, 275 reptiles, and 137 mammals, including 15 cats and dogs, pass through Heathrow Airport each day. Airline cargo compartments in which animals travel are temperature-controlled and pressurized for their well-being.

40 air traffic controllers work shifts around the clock to ensure the safety of planes during takeoff and landing.

A DAY OFF

WHAT DO YOU DO when you have time to yourself? Do you spring into action and ride off on your bike, or put on your in-line skates? Or do you do as little as possible and simply sit down in front of the tv, or lounge in the bathtub? Do you want to be thrilled and entertained at an amusement park or the movies? Do you travel the world and marvel at its wonders, from the mighty Grand Canyon to the Great Pyramid? Whatever you do, you will be surprised to discover how many other people are spending the day doing the same thing!

The Grand Canyon, Arizona, has 12,000 visitors a day.

The CN Tower, Toronto, Canada, attracts 5,000 visitors a day.

Kennedy Space Center, Florida, sells 1,500 tickets to admit visitors to watch the launch of the shuttle.

The Empire State Building, New York, attracts 7,000 visitors a day.

The Blackpool Tower, Blackpool, UK, draws 3,300 visitors a day.

Uluru (Ayers Rock), Northern Territory, Australia, has 900 visitors a day.

Stonehenge, Wiltshire, England, attracts 2,000 visitors a day.

Kew Gardens, London, England, has 2,700 visitors a day.

The Tower of London, London, UK, attracts 7,000 visitors a day.

The Eiffel Tower, Paris, France, attracts 15,000 visitors a day.

The Great Pyramid, Giza, Egypt, draws 10,000 visitors a day.

Old Faithful Geyser, Yellowstone National Park, has 8,000 visitors a day.

A day out, a night out

All the world loves a day out. Every day, 173,000 people visit America's National Parks. The world's most spectacular night out is offered by Monte Carlo. Every night for a week in July and August each year, as part of an international competition, 1.1 tons (1 tonne) of fireworks are launched into the skies above the Mediterranean harbor.

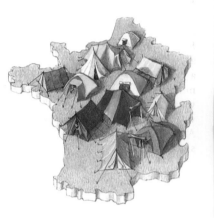

French camping

The French have a passion for camping, and an abundance of beautiful countryside in which to pitch their tents. Every night, nearly three million French people sleep under canvas.

Bombay

"Stop crackling that popadom, I can't hear the movie!"

Indian movies

India is the most film-loving nation in the world. It has 13,000 screens, including 4,000 mobile cinemas. Every day, 15 million Indians visit the movies. That's like having the whole population of Bombay, India's film-making capital, at the movie theater.

Universal Studios, California, draws 15,000 visitors a day.

The British Museum, London, England, has 17,000 visitors a day.

The Louvre Museum, Paris, France, attracts 17,000 visitors every day.

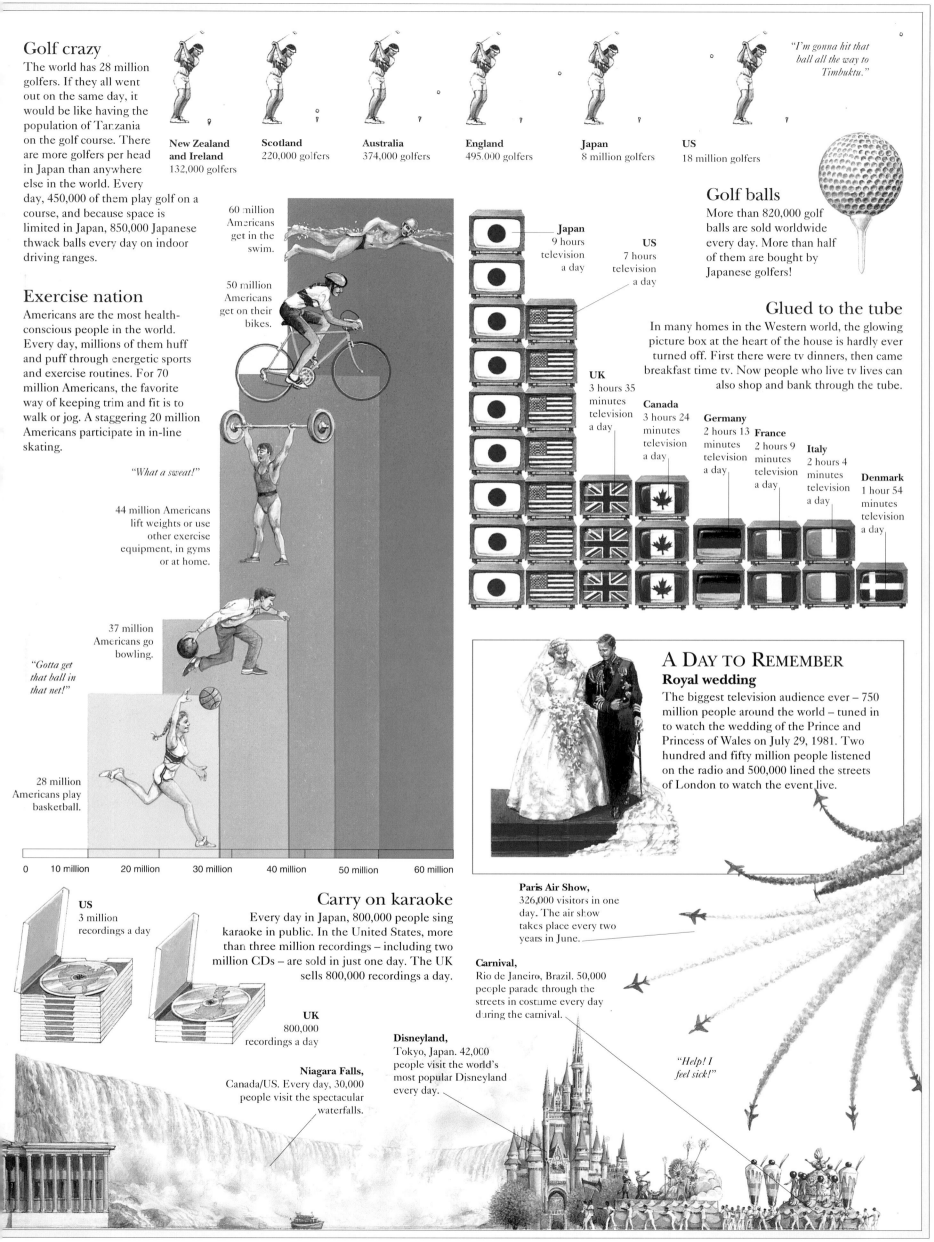

Golf crazy

The world has 28 million golfers. If they all went out on the same day, it would be like having the population of Tanzania on the golf course. There are more golfers per head in Japan than anywhere else in the world. Every day, 450,000 of them play golf on a course, and because space is limited in Japan, 850,000 Japanese thwack balls every day on indoor driving ranges.

"I'm gonna hit that ball all the way to Timbuktu."

New Zealand and Ireland 132,000 golfers

Scotland 220,000 golfers

Australia 374,000 golfers

England 495,000 golfers

Japan 8 million golfers

US 18 million golfers

Golf balls

More than 820,000 golf balls are sold worldwide every day. More than half of them are bought by Japanese golfers!

Exercise nation

Americans are the most health-conscious people in the world. Every day, millions of them huff and puff through energetic sports and exercise routines. For 70 million Americans, the favorite way of keeping trim and fit is to walk or jog. A staggering 20 million Americans participate in in-line skating.

60 million Americans get in the swim.

50 million Americans get on their bikes.

"What a sweat!"

44 million Americans lift weights or use other exercise equipment, in gyms or at home.

37 million Americans go bowling.

"Gotta get that ball in that net!"

28 million Americans play basketball.

0 | 10 million | 20 million | 30 million | 40 million | 50 million | 60 million

Glued to the tube

In many homes in the Western world, the glowing picture box at the heart of the house is hardly ever turned off. First there were tv dinners, then came breakfast time tv. Now people who live tv lives can also shop and bank through the tube.

Japan 9 hours television a day

US 7 hours television a day

UK 3 hours 35 minutes television a day

Canada 3 hours 24 minutes television a day

Germany 2 hours 13 minutes television a day

France 2 hours 9 minutes television a day

Italy 2 hours 4 minutes television a day

Denmark 1 hour 54 minutes television a day

A DAY TO REMEMBER
Royal wedding

The biggest television audience ever – 750 million people around the world – tuned in to watch the wedding of the Prince and Princess of Wales on July 29, 1981. Two hundred and fifty million people listened on the radio and 500,000 lined the streets of London to watch the event live.

Carry on karaoke

Every day in Japan, 800,000 people sing karaoke in public. In the United States, more than three million recordings – including two million CDs – are sold in just one day. The UK sells 800,000 recordings a day.

US 3 million recordings a day

UK 800,000 recordings a day

Paris Air Show, 326,000 visitors in one day. The air show takes place every two years in June.

Carnival, Rio de Janeiro, Brazil. 50,000 people parade through the streets in costume every day during the carnival.

Disneyland, Tokyo, Japan. 42,000 people visit the world's most popular Disneyland every day.

Niagara Falls, Canada/US. Every day, 30,000 people visit the spectacular waterfalls.

"Help! I feel sick!"

INDEX

A
acid rain, 25
aircraft, 21, 28
airlines, 21, 28, 29
airports, 28, 29
aluminum, 23, 25
anesthetic, 17
animals, 12, 15
armed forces, 7
astronauts, 6, 21, 26

B
bacteria, 17
balloons, 28
bamboo, 10
bats, 12, 13
beards, 16
bees, 12, 13
BiCs, 6, 27
bicycles, 7
Biosphere 2, 9
birds, 12, 13
birthdays, 19
births, 19
blinking, 16
blood, 16
body heat, 16
brain, 17
bread, 6, 21
breathing, 16

C
calories, 17, 20
camping, 30
cans, 25
cars, 22, 23, 24, 28
  battery-powered, 29
  breakdowns, 29
cement, 22
cereals, 21
cities, 18
clothing, 25
coal, 22
cocoa, 20
communications, 26, 27
computers, 23, 27
cosmic dust, 8
cotton, 7
crayons, 7
cryonics, 19

D
day, 8
deaths, 19
deforestation, 24
delivery services, 27
diamonds, 22
diapers, 24
digestive system, 16, 17
dreaming, 17

E
Earth, 8, 9
earthquakes, 9
eating, 12, 17
eggs, 20
electricity, 22
energy, 22, 24
erosion, 9
excrement, 17
extinct animals, 14

F
fairy rings, 11
farts, 17
fast food, 20
fireworks, 30
fish, 7, 21
flight, 12, 13
flowers, 10, 27
food, 12, 16, 17, 20, 21
fruit, 20, 21
fungi, 11

G
garlic, 21
garbage, 24
gas, 22
glaciers, 8, 9
global warming, 8, 9
golf, 31
greeting cards, 27

H
hailstones, 9
hair, 16
heartbeat, 12, 16
Heathrow Airport, 28, 29
helicopters, 28
honey, 21
household waste, 24
hovercraft, 28
human body, 16, 17
hurricanes, 9

I, K
ice, 9
insects, 12, 13
karaoke, 31
Kew Gardens, 11, 30
kidney, 16
kitchen appliances, 23, 25

L
languages, 27
leisure, 30, 31
lichens, 10, 11
lightning, 9
lungs, 16

M
machines, 22
mail, 27
manufacturing, 23
meat, 20
metals, 23
milk, 17
money, 23
Morse Code, 27
motorcycles, 28
music, 31

N, O
nails, 16, 17
newspapers, 24
oil, 11, 22
  spillages, 25
operations, 17

P
packaging, 24
paper, 24
parasites, 17
passports, 29
Pentagon, 27
photosynthesis, 9, 10
Pioneer 10, 26
plants, 10, 11
population, 7, 18, 19
production, 22, 23

R
radio telescope, 26
railroads, 7
rainfall, 9
recordings, 31
recycling, 24, 25
rice, 21

S
salivary glands, 16
salt, 20
satellites, 26, 27
SeaCat ferry, 28
sea dumping, 25
seaweed, 10
skin cells, 16
sleep, 15, 17
snakes, 7
snow, 9
soap powder, 23
space observatory, 26
space probe, 26
space shuttle, 26
space telescope, 27
speed (animals), 12
sperm, 16
sport, 6, 31
stamina (animals), 14
stamps, 27

(steel–swimming)
steel, 23, 25
stomach, 16
storms, 8, 9
string, 23
sugar, 21
Sun, 9, 10
sweat, 17
swimming, 13

T
taxis, 6
tea, 20
tears, 16
tectonic plates, 9
telephones, 6, 27
television, 31
temperature, 9
test tube baby, 19
timber, 23
tires, 23, 25
tourism, 29, 30, 31
toxic waste, 25
traffic jams, 29
trains, 28
transatlantic cable, 27
travel, 28, 29
trees, 10, 11, 24
tropical rain forest, 11, 24

U, V
urine, 17
vaccination, 17
vegetables, 20, 21
volcanoes, 7, 8

W, X
waste, 24, 25
water consumption, 24, 25
waterfalls, 9
weather, 9
weather forecasting, 26
weddings, 7, 19, 31
winds, 9
wine, 7
wings, 12, 13
wool, 7
X-rays, 17

ACKNOWLEDGMENTS

DK would like to thank the following people:
Illustrators: Richard Bonson, Stephen Conlin, Peter Dennis (Linda Rogers Associates), Chris Forsey, Malcolm Mcgregor, and Peter Visscher.
Editorial: Francesca Baines, Robert Graham, Angela Koo, Nichola Roberts.
Design: Simon Faiers
Index: Chris Bernstein
Additional Acknowledgments:
The Automobile Association, Biosphere II, Peter Bond, Gary Booth, Heathrow Airport, Kew Gardens, Keith Lye, Milton Keynes Recycling Facility, Royal Automobile Club, Royal Horticultural Society Library, Martin Walters, Richard Walters, World Resources Foundation.

Special thanks to Caroline Ash.